PAUL
GOD'S
ADVENTURER

PAUL
GOD'S ADVENTURER

Robbie Trent

WORD BOOKS
PUBLISHER
WACO, TEXAS

First Printing, July 1975
Second Printing, January 1976
First Paperback Printing, October 1978

Library of Congress catalog card number: 75-10089
ISBN 0-8499-2844-3
Printed in the United States of America

Illustrations by Ron Adair

Contents

Preface

This book is about Paul the Apostle. Designed for young and old, it is a most valuable and helpful guide in depicting the whole career of this "adventurer of Christ."

I have been honored to check this book for accuracy on archaeological details; thus I have made a few suggestions concerning this area of research.

Paul is not only one of the central figures in religious history; he is a central figure in world history. There is no real way to appreciate Paul's life and contribution apart from his transforming rebirth experience. It ought to occasion no surprise, therefore, that Paul recounts it so frequently in the New Testament. He must have related his conversion experience in most of his spoken sermons, and there must have been many such instances of which we have no present record.

The "light" that scattered Paul's spiritual blindness on the road to Damascus continued to serve Paul as the "light" which directed him in world-wide missionary service.

JERRY VARDAMAN

Foreword

This is the story of Paul, the Apostle to the Gentiles, the man who produced the largest number of books of all the New Testament writers. It is the story, too, of Saul of Tarsus, the man who once hated Christianity so much that he hunted down the followers of Christ even to their death. It is the story of a man God changed, and who, in turn, changed the thinking of people over most of the world of his day.

To understand how much Saul himself was changed, it is necessary to look at some of the training and experiences that entered into his childhood and made him a fierce opponent of the followers of Jesus of Nazareth.

On the childhood of Saul, the Bible is silent. Why? Because the Bible is the story of God's revelation of himself, especially in Jesus Christ. Its writers were seeking to pass on that revelation and chose their materials well.

This book you are reading seeks to interpret the man Paul. Since childhood experiences entered into making him the man he was, it uses them.

Looking at these experiences can help us to understand the man who first appears in the Bible when the martyr Stephen was stoned. Saul's life, before that time, must be constructed from his background

which is indicated in his own statements in the
Bible:

> I am a Jew, born in Tarsus of Cilicia, a
> citizen of an important city.[1]
> I am a Jew, born in Tarsus of Cilicia, but
> brought up here in Jerusalem as a student of
> Gamaliel. I received strict instruction in the
> Law of our ancestors, and was just as dedi-
> cated to God as all of you here today are.[2]
> I was free born.[3]
> I was ahead of most fellow Jews of my age
> in my practice of the Jewish religion. I was
> much more devoted to the traditions of our an-
> cestors.[4]

The Bible indicates that this same Paul, first called
Saul, was trained in the craft of tentmaking and
spoke in the Hebrew, Greek, and Aramaic languages.
There are also evidences that he was acquainted
with Latin.

What was the man Paul really like? How did he
feel about things? How did he think? To answer
these questions we must consider the geography, history, and customs of the first century A.D. when he
lived. We must think of the home and city in which
he grew up.

As the son of a Pharisee, Saul would be reared
strictly according to Jewish laws and customs. As a
native of Tarsus, a city in Cilicia, he would be ex-
posed to Greek culture, Greek customs, and some
Greek people. All these facts about his background
are evident in his letters. Since Saul's father was also
a Roman citizen, the family would have some standing in the community.

As a boy, Saul would have the urges and ambitions,

the problems and interests, the thirst for discovery, and the tendency to investigate that belong to an intelligent, growing child in all ages and cultures.

As the writer of this book, I hope that seeing Saul of Tarsus against the background and customs of his childhood may help you to have a new appreciation of him as a man and as the great Christian he became. The first seven chapters, therefore, try to picture what Paul's childhood and early manhood must have been. The happenings used might have been typical for any well-trained Jewish boy who lived in Tarsus in the first century A.D.

Chapter 8 includes the stoning of Stephen, and, along with the remaining chapters, centers on events reported in the Book of Acts and in Paul's letters.

Because the materials in these first chapters gave me an increasing appreciation of Paul, I hope that you will read them along with the rest of the book.

ROBBIE TRENT

ACTS 21:39; 22:3; 28; GALATIANS 1:14

I.
The Boy Saul

"Don't let them do it, Mother!" Saul panted as he ran into the room and found his mother setting out bread for the evening meal.

She turned and looked at him.

"Get your breath, my son," she said. "Then tell me what you are talking about."

Saul sat down, but he was trembling.

"The river," he explained. "Apollonius says they are moving the river."

"You must be mistaken, my son," his mother said as she wiped the tears and dust from Saul's face. "The Cydnus River has flowed through the middle of Tarsus all the years I have lived here and long before. Men cannot move a river."

"I saw them, Mother. Apollonius and I saw the men digging and piling rocks as tall as the mountains. Already the stream in the city is smaller."

"You have displeased me again, Saul," his mother shook her head. "I do not like for you to associate with Apollonius. He is not a Jew but a Greek, and your father would be distressed that you have played with him again."

"Must Father know?" Saul asked.

His mother considered for a moment. "It is your sixth birthday," she said at last. "Unless your father asks, we will not mention Apollonius today. Come

13

and help me spread a fresh cloth for our evening meal. I believe you are tall enough to light the candles of joy."

"I am glad my birthday came on the sabbath day," Saul said. "The candles make it almost like a feast."

Saul knew that the Jewish sabbath began at sunset on Friday. Soon Father would come home. He was never late for the sabbath meal.

The sun was low in the sky when Saul's father entered the door.

"I am later than usual," he explained, "but I went by the river."

"The river?" Saul ran to him. "Are they really moving the river?"

"So it seems, my son. The emperor has ordered the new channel dug east of the city so that the waters of the Cydnus will no longer overflow into the streets. There will be only small streams in the city."

"What about the ships?" Saul questioned. "Where will they go?"

"Many of them will continue to sail up the river from the port of Rhegma less than ten miles away," his father explained. "There is the sea, the blue Mediterranean. Someday I will take you to see the sea and the ships."

"Now?" Saul questioned.

"Not now," his mother interrupted. "Now it is time to eat our sabbath evening meal."

Carefully Saul's father poured water over his hands three times, for this was a religious rule of a good Jew.

The table was ready, and Saul stood on tiptoe to light the two tall candles.

His lips moved but made no sound as his father repeated the first mealtime prayer:

"Blessed art thou, O Lord, King of the universe, who hast brought forth bread out of the earth. Blessed be he who giveth food to all."

Together mother and father and son ate the lamb stew and the cakes made from meal which the boy had helped his mother grind the day before. There was a special treat tonight. Mother had let Saul gather ripe figs from the tree which grew in the yard.

When supper was finished, Saul's father said, "Let us bless God of whose bounty we have eaten."

Young Saul and his mother replied, "Blessed be he of whose bounty we have eaten and by whose goodness we live."

Then Saul and his father climbed the outside steps to the roof, and together they looked at the nighttime sky.

"Blessed art thou, O Lord, who hast made creation," Saul heard his father say.

"Tell me about the stars," Saul begged, and his father told him in words which Saul had heard so often that he could repeat them by himself.

In the beginning God created the heavens and the earth. . . . And God made the two great lights, the greater light to rule the day, and the lesser light to rule the night; he made the stars also.

And God set them in the firmament of the heavens to give light upon the earth, to rule over the day and over the night, and to separate the light from the darkness. And God saw that it was good.[5]

Saul was quiet for a moment. Then, because he loved to hear his father's voice, he said, "Tell me what my name means."

"Saul means 'asked of God,'" his father replied.
"It was the name of Israel's first king who stood tall
and straight. You have a Roman name too, the name
Paul."

"Apollonius calls me Paul sometimes," Saul told
his father, but clapped his hand over his mouth, for
he had not meant to mention Apollonius.

"You have seen Apollonius again?" his father questioned.

Saul nodded. "Yes," he admitted. "He showed me
how men are moving the river."

"What do you and Apollonius talk about?" Saul's
father asked.

"Many things," Saul replied. "Today he asked me
about the blue thread in the bottom of my coat."

"What did you tell him, my son?"

"I told him of the words of Moses when he gave
God's command to our people to put a blue cord in
the fringe of their coats to remind them of God's
commands which they must obey."

"That was a good answer, my son. You must never
forget that you are a Jew.

"I would have you play with boys who are Jewish,
not with a heathen Greek."

"I like Apollonius, Father," Saul said. "Why can
I not play with him? He shows me beautiful things,
and he speaks of the wonders of the sun and the
moon and the stars. His father taught him about
them."

Saul's father repeated an old saying of the Jews,
"Cursed be he who feeds swine: And cursed be he
who teaches his son Greek literature."

Saul was startled at the hate in his father's voice
as he continued.

"You know that Apollonius is a Greek. His people worship false gods; they eat strange foods. They were not chosen of the Jehovah God as the Jews were. You must never enter the house of a Greek or touch his food. You must not listen to his tales."

Saul was silent for a minute. Then he changed the subject by asking, "Does my Roman name have a meaning too?"

"A Roman name is honored," his father replied. "You are a free-born Roman citizen as well as a Jew. I too am a Roman citizen. The laws of Rome forbid that a citizen be whipped without a trial. They give him the privilege of appealing any ruling of the court to the emperor in Rome."

"Yes, Father," Saul murmured. Rome and Roman laws seemed very far away and not very interesting.

"You are getting sleepy," his father said. "Let us repeat the Shema together before we go to bed."

Saul's father lifted his eyes to the skies, and the boy's sleepy voice joined in as they repeated the words:

Hear, O Israel: The Lord our God is one Lord; and you shall love the Lord your God with all your heart, and with all your soul, and with all your might.[6]

Saul knew that these words were in a little case on the doorpost of every devout Jew.

Before they entered the door, both Father and Son touched the mezuzah on the doorpost. Then they went inside the house.

Saul lay down upon his mat. He heard the chirp of crickets. He closed his eyes, and the sound grew fainter and fainter. Saul was asleep.

2.
Sabbath Day

A thin thread of light was shining under the door when Saul opened his eyes the next day. Sleepily the boy repeated the words he had said every morning since he could remember:

> I thank thee, O living and eternal king,
> That thou hast graciously restored my soul to me;
> Great is thy faithfulness.

And he added,

> Moses commanded us a law,
> An inheritance of the congregation of Jacob.

Saul didn't exactly understand the prayer or what "an inheritance of the congregation of Jacob" meant. Neither was he quite sure why he was not allowed to speak the name of God until after he had washed his hands. He did understand that this was a Jewish rule, and he knew that Jewish rules must not be broken. They had become a part of the Holy Law itself.

Saul thought about those many rules as he poured water first over one hand three times and then over the other hand three times. That, too, was one of the rules and a part of the Law. Saul wondered whether he would ever learn all of those rules. His

18

father knew them all and prided himself on obeying every one of them. For his father was a good Pharisee.

Saul washed his face and got ready to go to the synagogue with his father and mother. This was the sabbath day.

Saul saw his father wind the phylactery around his arm and put the frontlet across his forehead. Even without looking, he knew that the markings on them were words from the Law of Moses.

Soon Saul and his mother and father were walking down the street. Saul was proud to be big enough to carry his father's scroll on which were written the prayers to be used in the synagogue.

"Will we hear from Jacob today?" Saul asked.

"Perhaps," his father replied. "Jacob is very sick and his pain is bad."

Would his friend Jacob be well soon? Saul wondered. Jacob had cut his knee when he fell, and the oil and wine which the doctor had poured on the wound had not made it heal.

The hill on which the synagogue stood was in sight now. "There is the House of the Book," Saul's father said, and Saul knew that the Book meant the scrolls of Holy Law.

The family climbed to the top of the hill. There they stopped to rest a moment.

Far away Saul could see the river rushing over the rocks, and beyond, the Taurus Mountains. Something moved.

"Look in that tree!" Saul exclaimed, as he pointed to a scarlet bird, but his father replied, "It is time to go inside. The service is about to begin."

His mother went to sit with the women on one

side of the synagogue. Saul and his father put on
their caps and walked to a low stone bench on the
other side. Saul gave the scroll of prayers to his
father. He looked at the steady flame of the lamp,
always burning to remind the people of the presence
of the one eternal God whom they worshiped.

Saul watched as the leader of the synagogue
service pushed back the curtains which hid the
scrolls of the Law in an open chest. The service had
begun.

The leader began to repeat a psalm, and the men
and women said it with him. When they repeated
the Shema, Saul too joined in, for he knew every
word:

> Hear, O Israel: The Lord our God is one Lord;
> and you shall love the Lord your God with all
> your heart, and with all your soul, and with all
> your might.[7]

Next came the eighteen blessings. At the end of
each one Saul said, "Amen." He tried to make the
word sound deep and loud just as it did when his
father repeated it.

Carefully the leader of the synagogue lifted a scroll
from the chest and gave it to the reader for the day.

The reader carried it to a high desk and unrolled
it until he found the place he wanted. He began to
read.

There were verses from the Law and verses from
the prophets. The speaker's voice went up and down,
up and down. Sometimes it sounded like the buzzing
of a great fly, and Saul found himself growing sleepy.
He sat up very straight and tried to listen to the
sermon which followed.

It was easier to keep awake when the announcements were made, for Saul recognized the names of some of the people mentioned.

"Jacob, son of Isaac, is still in pain," the leader said. "He has a high fever."

Saul pulled at his father's arm. "Why don't they take the sap of the balsam tree and make a salve to ease the pain?" he whispered.

His father frowned and shook his head. "Don't talk now," he warned.

Saul did not speak again, but he kept on thinking about his friend Jacob.

On the way home, Saul was still thinking about Jacob. Suddenly he had an idea. "We have a balsam tree," he said aloud. "Why can't we make a salve from the sap and take it to Jacob this afternoon? It would help him."

"On sabbath day!" Father almost shouted the words. "Mixing medicine is work. And work is forbidden on the sabbath."

Mother nodded. "Jacob lives more than two miles away," she said. "The Law says we can travel only a bit more than a mile on sabbath day. Nor can we lift a burden, not even one so small as a package of medicine."

"Not even to ease pain?" Saul asked.

"Not for any cause," his father replied firmly.

Saul did not say more.

That afternoon a neighbor came running to the house of Saul. "My ox has fallen into a deep ditch," he said. "I think he has broken his leg. Come and help me lift him out. That ox cost me much money."

Saul's father went at once.

"Isn't an ox a burden?" Saul asked his mother. "Why can we lift him out of the ditch, yet we must not take medicine to Jacob?"

His mother shook her head.

"You ask too many questions."

She waited a moment, and then she turned to Saul and smiled. "Would you like a story?" she asked.

"Oh yes," Saul answered. "I love for you to tell me stories."

The door was shaded by a tree, so mother and son sat on the steps. Saul put his head on her knee and closed his eyes.

"A long time ago," the story began.

Saul drew a deep breath. He knew the story that his mother began that way, and he never tired of hearing it.

"A long time ago," his mother said, "your ancestor Abraham heard the voice of the Lord God speaking to him.

" 'Abraham,' God said, 'leave your home here in the land of Chaldea and go on a long journey. I will show you where to go. I will be near to help you as you travel.

" 'Leave your home and your father and your kin-folk and go to a land which I will show you. Do this, and I will make your name honored.

" 'You will be a blessing to many people, and I will make your descendants a great nation.'

"Abraham did just as God said. He took his wife, and his camels, his sheep, and all his other animals, his servants, and all the possessions he could carry.

"It was a long, long journey, but Abraham trusted God to keep his promise.

"And God did. They came at last to the land of Canaan. There Abraham's sons and grandsons and their sons were born and grew up."

Saul opened his eyes.

"One grandson was named Israel," he interrupted.

His mother nodded.

"Yes," she agreed. "That was the new name God's messenger gave to Jacob, son of Isaac, one night when Jacob found that God was very near. So close did God seem that Jacob said, 'I have seen God face to face.' "

His mother stopped for a moment, and Saul went on with the story.

"That is why we Jews are called Israelites. Israel had twelve sons, and we are their descendants. Our family comes from the honored tribe of Benjamin who was Jacob's youngest son."

"Very good, my son," his mother said.

Saul waited a moment. Then he asked a question. "Mother, why is a great nation like ours ruled by foreign Romans?"

His mother shook her head.

"I do not know, my son, but God has promised that someday he will send the Messiah to deliver Israel. For his coming we wait."

It was almost dark when Saul's father returned. There was no time for talk. There was only time for the prayers which marked the close of the sabbath day at sunset.

3.
School Days in Tarsus

"It's time to get up." Saul awoke with a start as he heard his mother's voice. He half opened his sleepy eyes. "It's still dark," he murmured.

"Yes, it's still dark," his mother agreed cheerfully, "but you start to school today, and school begins at six o'clock this time of year, you remember."

Saul jumped from his sleeping mat. He repeated his morning prayer and ran to wash his hands. He must wait for breakfast until school was over at ten o'clock, but he talked as he got ready to go.

"What will I learn at synagogue school, Father?" he wanted to know.

"You will study the Law, my son. You will learn to read and to write our Hebrew language. You will learn the history of our people and the dealings of God with them."

"I know the way to the synagogue." Saul offered this bit of information in the hope that he might be allowed to go by himself.

His father smiled. "I am sure you know the way," he agreed, "but the slave Gracios will walk with you."

Saul did not argue. He liked Gracios, the Greek, but he also liked to do things all by himself. Yet he knew he must do as his father said. Soon the two set out.

"I have been to the synagogue with my father many

times on sabbath day," he told Gracios as they climbed the hill.

"I am sure you have," Gracios replied, "but today is different. This is your first day at school."

"Do you think I really will learn to know the Law as well as my father does?" Saul asked.

"To possess such knowledge takes many years," Gracios explained, "but today you can begin. Here we are at the door. I must leave you now."

Before he went inside the synagogue, Saul took off his sandals. When he entered the room, he saw that some of his friends were already in the group—Jacob, and Jonathan, and Hiram.

Saul folded his coat to make a mat to sit on, and then he joined the group. Now there were fifteen boys seated in the half circle on the floor. They looked up at the rabbi who would be their teacher. He sat on a low seat facing them.

The teacher lifted the scroll of the Law which he had placed on a table before him. He pointed to a verse and read it in Hebrew. Then he repeated it in Aramaic, since many Jewish boys of the first century A.D. spoke Aramaic as well as Hebrew.

The rabbi repeated the verse again in Hebrew, and Saul and the other boys said the words after him at the top of their voices. This they would do every day until they had memorized every word of the first five books of the Old Testament—and even more.

When the group could repeat a verse, the teacher pointed to a letter of one of the words. He said the name of the letter and copied it on a small wax tablet with a stylus, a pencil-like stick. Then he called the names of the boys one by one.

Each boy in turn took the stylus in his own hand.

The teacher put his hand over the boy's and guided it around the outline of the letter.

"What does the word mean?" Saul asked as his small fingers grasped the stylus.

"You will learn that later," the rabbi answered. "First you must learn to repeat every Law, word for word. You must learn to write each one."

Saul tried very hard to retrace the letter, but his fingers cramped from the unusual task. He was hungry, and his legs ached to run outdoors. He was glad when ten o'clock came and it was time to go home.

His mother was waiting at the door. She poured a glass of goat's milk for him and gave him some dried dates.

"What did you do at school today?" she asked.

Saul swallowed the last drop of his milk and ate the last date before he answered. "We copied a verse from the scroll of Leviticus," he said with pride.

His mother nodded. "Yes," she said, "I have heard that the Laws of Leviticus are the first to be taught to boys in the synagogue school. Soon you will be able to write a verse all by yourself."

"The rabbi repeated some rules that do not seem good." Saul spoke slowly. "Is it good to hate?"

"It is said that the voice of the rabbi is the voice of God," his mother replied.

"What is the Law, Mother?" Saul asked.

"It is the will of God declared in the first five books of the Scriptures," his mother replied. "In a few years you will know every word and every letter of those first five books. Today your father bought you a stylus of your very own."

That afternoon, when Mother was busy, Saul

slipped away to show the stylus to Apollonius and to tell him about his important day. Together the two boys sat in the shade of a tamarisk tree and talked.

Apollonius listened politely as Saul told of school in the synagogue and explained that *synagogue* meant "House of the Book."

"I know," Apollonius said, "my teacher told me."

"Do Greeks know about the ways of the Jews?" Saul asked in amazement. And he added, "Tell me about your school. What do you study?"

"When I was about your age, I learned to read and to write and to do arithmetic problems," Apollonius explained. "Now that I am older, I go to the university. I will take you there someday. In addition to the Greek language, we study the wise sayings of the philosophers, and we learn to think about what they mean. We study the moon and the stars and the ways of beauty. We study music and dancing. We train our bodies to be strong. We play games that develop strength and skill."

Saul sighed. He wished his school taught games, but he did not say so. "Of course Hebrew and the Law are more important," he said firmly.

"All knowledge is important," Apollonius replied politely, and the boys spoke of other things.

Saul asked his father about some of the things Apollonius had mentioned as they sat on the rooftop together that night. "Will I learn about beauty and music at school?" he asked.

"No," his father replied. "You study only important things at the synagogue. In addition to reading and writing Hebrew, you will learn the Law and the history of the Jewish people."

"I already know something about our people," Saul boasted. "Mother has told me about them."

"Yes," his father agreed, "but you will learn more."

The next day he gave young Saul a small scroll containing the Shema, the Ten Commandments, and some of the psalms of praise to God. Saul was proud to carry it to school with him.

He learned quickly. In the synagogue there were four groups of boys: those who were quick to learn and quick to forget; those who were slow to learn and slow to forget; those who were quick to learn and slow to forget; and those who were slow to learn and quick to forget. Saul and three of his friends made up the third group. They learned quickly, and they seemed to remember all that they learned. More and more hours were spent in school. At some seasons of the year, the pupils stayed at the synagogue all day. And there were no vacations.

As months went by, Saul grew tired of the monotony of learning to repeat the Hebrew words of the Law and to draw the strange Hebrew letters. Often, as he saw the heavily laden mules bring in lead and silver from the mines of Cilicia, he wished he knew what lay beyond the mountains.

Springtime came and with it the season of the famous Greek games.

"Come and see the great race with me," Apollonius invited Saul one day, and Saul slipped away from school to go. What he was doing nagged at his mind at first, and he felt uncomfortable until the race began. Then he forgot everything but the running.

Tall, graceful young men lined up at the starting post. At the signal, they began to run with all their might. Saul watched one boy in particular. The muscles in his legs were large and strong. He ran quickly at first, then more slowly for a time. Later Saul saw him increase his speed until at last he reached the goal. He stood proudly before the judges and bent his head to receive the crown of laurel leaves, the reward of the victor.

At school the next day the teacher asked Saul why he had been absent. Saul had known the question would come, and he had thought of saying he had been sick. But Saul was too proud to lie.

"I was watching the Greek race," he admitted and took his punishment.

Months and years went by. Sometimes, when school was over early, Saul went with Apollonius to hear the philosophers who spoke daily in a shady spot near an old Greek temple. He was fascinated. He admired the sculptured stones in spite of his Jewish prejudice against carved figures. His eyes drank in the beauty of form and design.

Listening to the philosophers made Saul think, for they asked questions. They spoke of the world of science, of literature, of art, and of music. One day a philosopher repeated words from one of the Greek poets. The poem was about a god of the Greeks, and all his life Saul remembered one of its lines, "In him we live and move and have our being."

Whenever he could, young Saul slipped away with his friend to hear talk of the wonders of thought and reasoning. "Someday I will learn about everything," Saul promised himself.

Before he was twelve years old, Saul could repeat

every word of the five books of the Law. He knew much of Jewish history. Of course he could read and write Hebrew as well as Aramaic.

"You must also learn to work with your hands," his father told him. "Every man must be able to make his own living. Would you like to learn to weave tents before you go to school in Jerusalem?"

Saul looked up with excitement. It was the ambition of every Jewish boy to see Jerusalem and go to school there. Even if he became a rabbi, he would need a trade by which to earn a living. For no rabbi was paid a salary for teaching. Weaving might be interesting too, he decided. He knew some of the weavers in Tarsus, and they had often told him tales of the sea and of faraway places.

With two upright beams, Saul's father helped him make a loom. Then he took him to an old weaver for instruction. Cilicia was famous for its goat's hair, and Saul knew that soon after shearing time the markets were piled high with the corded and spun goat's hair yarn. Saul learned to choose the best yarn and to argue with the merchant until he agreed to what Saul thought a good price. His nimble fingers were soon threading the warp quickly and evenly on the loom. Even more quickly they were throwing the shuttle which carried the thread over and under the warp to make the woof. Saul knew that goat's hair which was old made darker thread, and the fresher hair could be used for lighter patterns. He took pride in his work and did it carefully. He became known for his good workmanship.

One day, almost without thinking, Saul wove into the tent cloth a design that looked a bit like the pillars of a Greek temple. Startled at what he had done, he unraveled the thread, for he knew that a Greek design would offend his father. The lighter threads had looked pretty on the darker ones, and Saul sighed as he unraveled the cloth. Apollonius would have liked the design, Saul knew.

But Saul was trying not to think about Apollonius these days. He was trying to hate everything that was not Jewish. His teachers said he must do that, and Saul was seeking to obey. But he could not hate Apollonius.

"When you are thirteen years old, you will be a Son of the Commandments," his father reminded him one night. "Then you will be going to Jerusalem."

"For the Passover?" Saul asked.

"For that and perhaps for something else," his father replied.

4.
Son of the Commandments

Days, weeks, months, and seasons went by—even years. Young Saul had learned all that the synagogue school in Tarsus could teach him. He could repeat, word for word, all the stories and verses in the scrolls of Genesis, Exodus, Leviticus, Numbers, and Deuteronomy. In addition, he knew many of the psalms and long passages from the prophets and the books of ancient wisdom—the "Sayings." He knew the Jewish rules about food and about health and cleanliness. He knew, too, many of the ceremonies that went with washing the hands for fear that they might have touched an object contaminated by contact with a person who was not a Jew—a Gentile.

Saul could recount the history of his people from Abraham on down through Joseph and the tribe of Benjamin. He knew, too, the responsibilities that were his as a Jew. He would accept these formally when he was thirteen years old.

Yet, deep in his heart, Saul knew something else. He realized that there were many, many things about which his school had taught him nothing. When he passed the famous Greek university in Tarsus, he often caught glimpses of beautiful buildings and shady groves where professors led their students to think about art and music and philosophy and all that was then known about the world and the wonders of nature. He saw statues of men whom the Greeks called great. Saul shuddered, for his father had told him these statues were idols.

One day as Saul walked with Apollonius down by the river, they saw ships with strange figures carved and painted on them. They saw one ship with a pair of scales painted on its prow and another with a carved, graceful figure of a youth. The young man represented the sun god Apollo, Apollonius told Saul.

"Why do they put such figures on their ships?" Saul asked. And Apollonius explained that the sailors thought such markings would bring good luck.

"Where do the ships come from?" Saul wanted to know.

"From Tyre and Rome and Egypt and other faraway places," Apollonius explained. "Some of them come from Greece, the land of my fathers. Did your teachers not tell you of these countries?"

Saul shook his head. "We studied the Law of God," he almost shouted. "That is the only thing important to a Jew."

Apollonius was quiet for a moment. Then he asked gently, "What really is a Jew? How does he differ from a Greek? I know a bit of history, and here in Tarsus are many Jewish people. They have hands and arms and eyes and ears just as I do. They must eat and drink just as I do. But most of these Jewish people are not friendly to me."

Saul was proud to tell about his people. He told Apollonius about Abraham and the promise that God would make of his descendants a great nation. He told of the ancient operation of circumcision which the Jewish Law ordered for every Jewish boy baby. "It means that he belongs to God's chosen people and must live by their Laws," he explained.

Saul spoke of the days of Solomon when the Jewish nation was rich and powerful. "The country was then called Israel," Saul explained. "That is why we Jews are sometimes called Israelites."

"That was a long time ago," Apollonius said. And Saul told him of the promise of God that the Jews would someday be a great nation again.

Apollonius was puzzled. "Your people have been conquered just as we Greeks have," he argued. "You live under Roman rule and pay taxes to the Roman government."

"Someday a new leader will come," Saul said confidently. "God has promised a Messiah who will deliver us from the Romans and lead us to the victory that belongs to the chosen people of God."

The ships had docked now, and Saul and Apollonius ran down to the water.

"Maybe some of the sailors will tell us about the sea and the lands they have visited," Saul said.

The boys were not disappointed. One man seated himself on the dock and leaned back against a post to watch the unloading.

He reminded the boys that once Mark Antony had lived in the Roman palace in Tarsus.

"When I was a boy," he said, "Queen Cleopatra of Egypt sailed into this very port. I saw the barge on which she sat. It was covered with gold, and the oars were made of silver. The sails were purple linen.

"All of Tarsus saw the queen on a couch on the deck with boys fanning her and maids hovering near to wait on her."

"Do the Romans rule in Egypt too?" Saul asked. "I have dropped anchor in many a port," the old man replied, "in Sicily, in Greece, wherever the Mediterranean touches, and in every place, the Romans rule."

The sailor went on to tell the boys about Rome and the palace of the Caesar and the great amphitheater where gladiators fought each other for the amusement of the people. He told of the sea and the huge white-foamed waves that thrust themselves up higher than the tallest building in Tarsus.

"I wish I could see everything," Saul told Apollonius. "Someday I will go to Rome."

The old man had finished his story now, and Saul and Apollonius started back into the city. Far away they could see the mountains and catch a glimpse of whiteness which meant rushing waters that filled the river and went on down to the sea. The mountains reminded Saul of a psalm he had learned which began: "I will lift up mine eyes unto the hills." He repeated the words aloud, and Apollonius said, "It sounds like a poem. You never told me that the Jews had poetry, Saul."

"I didn't think of it as a poem," Saul replied. "It is really a prayer."

"I like the part that says your God does not go to sleep but always keeps watch," Apollonius said. "I wish our Greek gods were like that. What are the words, Saul?"

"He that keepeth Israel shall neither slumber nor sleep," Saul repeated. Then he added, "It is God's promise to his people, the Jews. We are Israel."

Apollonius did not speak for some time. Then he said, "I must go now. I promised to be home early."

He waved good-by to Saul.

Saul waved back. Then he turned and stood for a moment looking at the sun setting over the water.

"Good-by, river," he said softly. "Someday I will know more about rivers and ride on a ship that sails the waters of the sea."

It was weeks later, on his birthday, that Saul formally became "a Son of the Commandments." His father told him of the ancient initiation into the tribe of Benjamin and gave him that tribe's special blessing:

> The beloved of the Lord shall dwell in safety
> by him; and the Lord shall cover him all the
> day long, and he shall dwell between his shoulders.[8]

"Between his shoulders?" Saul repeated the words questioningly.

"Very near to his heart," his father explained, "in the very safest place."

Later, in the synagogue, Saul repeated long passages of the Law which he had memorized, and the older men gave him their blessing.

"I am now a Son of the Commandments," Saul announced to his mother the next day. "Soon I will be going to Jerusalem with Father to celebrate the Passover."

She did not look at her son.

"Yes," she replied, "I am preparing for that."

Saul noticed that she was sewing and washing and ironing and mending more than usual, but he thought little about it until the day before he and his father were to leave for the Passover. Then he saw his mother folding all his coats and tunics carefully and making them into a bundle.

"I won't need all those clothes, Mother," Saul told her. "We won't be away long."

His father too had been watching. He turned to Saul.

"We will observe the Passover together in Jerusalem," he told his son. "Then I will return to Tarsus. You will remain in Jerusalem to study there."

Saul gasped in surprise. He was to study in Jerusalem with the great rabbis there! Maybe he would learn about the world as Apollonius had done in the university at Tarsus.

"How will we go to Jerusalem?" he asked his father. "Over the mountains and across Cilicia and then down the shore and across to Judea?"

His father shook his head. "A trading ship from Tyre is leaving the port for Caesarea," he explained. "We will sail on that ship and from Caesarea go by land with other Passover pilgrims to Jerusalem."

"Go on a ship!" Saul stared at his father in amazement. He remembered the strange emblems on the vessels he had seen. He knew that the sailors were heathen.

"Yes," his father replied. "That is one reason your mother is packing so many cakes and dried dates. We must carry food with us. We must also take skins of wine, for there will be no fresh water until we reach Caesarea."

"Travel on the sea!" Saul whispered the words in wonder. He had never dreamed of such a voyage on the way to Jerusalem. The trip would be almost as exciting as the Temple and the city itself.

Saul was so busy with thoughts of the new experiences that were before him that he told his mother good-by with little concern for the many days that would pass before he saw her again. She dried her eyes so that he would not know that she had been thinking of them and crying.

Saul and his father started down the street. Before they reached the corner, Saul turned and looked back. He could see his mother standing in the doorway. She was waving her hand.

Saul waved back. Then he and his father went down another street and left Tarsus.

On they walked, to the harbor at Rhegma on the coast of Cilicia.

PSALM 107:23–26, 28–30; 147:1, 4–5;
EZEKIEL 27:2–9

5.
On the Sea

The ship which Saul and his father boarded was
a small freighter carrying lumber. It would stay as
close as possible to the coast.

Saul watched as the sailors unfurled the sails to
catch the breeze. He saw scantily dressed men take
their places at the long oars. He watched others
loosen the ropes and draw up the anchor. He heard
the sound of song as the half-naked slaves grasped
the oars and began to row. The ship pulled away from
the dock.

Soon Saul could no longer see the harbor on the
coastline of Cilicia. Then even the Taurus Mountains
faded away. The ship was in the open Mediterranean
now, and, as far as Saul could see, there was nothing
in sight but water and sky. Sometimes in the clear
blue water, Saul saw a fish.

Often, when darkness came, Saul and his father
looked up at the sky, and Saul wondered about the
moon and the stars.

His father pointed out Orion, and Saul remembered that Apollonius had called the constellation
"the hunter" and told him the story of the Greek goddess Artemis. He remembered, too, words his mother
had repeated to him one night as they sat together on
the housetop.

41

It is good to sing praise to our God; . . .
He has determined the number of the stars
and calls each one by name.
Great and almighty is our Lord.[9]

How many stars were there, Saul wondered.

Saul asked his father many questions. How did the sailors know they could steer by the North Star? How large was the sea? How many lands did it touch? What made the waves roll and fall?

Saul's father could not answer. He knew little of the ways of the sea. The Jews were not a seagoing people and traveled little on the water.

The sailors had little time to talk, and Saul's father did not encourage conversation with them. "The men who row are slaves," he explained. "They are ignorant and know only how to handle an oar."

That job they knew and did well.

How Saul wished for Apollonius! He would have loved the trip and might have known answers to some of Saul's questions.

When Saul pointed to a high wave one day, his father reminded him of the time centuries before when God had divided the waters of another sea, and Moses had led the Israelites to pass through it on a dry path between the walls of water.

From the stories his mother had told him, Saul remembered that years afterwards King Solomon had a great fleet of ships which carried gold and silver and ivory and apes and peacocks across the sea to the land of Israel. Then, he recalled, silver had been as plentiful as cobblestones in the streets of Jerusalem.

"The Lord made Solomon rich and great," his father reminded him. " 'The Lord is a great God and a great king above all gods.' " Both of them looked at

the strange carvings on the prow of the ship, and his
father added, "The sea is his, and he made it."

One day Saul pointed out dark clouds filling the
sky. He saw the sailors shake their heads and heard
them mutter that a storm was coming.

The winds blew hard, and the waves rushed higher
and higher. To Saul they looked like angry, towering
mountains. He was afraid.

Then he felt his father's hand on his shoulder and
heard his father's voice, clear and steady, as he repeated a psalm that Saul had learned in synagogue
school.

> Some sailed over the ocean in ships,
>   earning their living on the seas;
> they saw what the Lord has done,
>   his wonderful acts on the seas.
> He commanded, and a mighty wind began to
>   blow and stirred up the waves.
> The ships were lifted high in the air and
>   plunged down into the depths; . . .
> In their trouble they called to the Lord,
>   and he saved them from their distress.
> He made the storm be still,
>   and the waves became quiet.
> They were glad because of the calm,
>   and he brought them safe to the port they
>   wanted.[10]

Soon the storm was over.

"We are nearing land," a sailor explained. "The
winds rush down out of the mountains."

"What mountains?" Saul asked.

"The mountains of Lebanon," the sailor replied.

"Mother told me about those mountains," Saul said
proudly. "King David had a palace built from cedars

that grew there. And Solomon brought timber from those same mountains for the first temple in Jerusalem."

Saul's father beamed with pride that his son remembered the history of his people so well. "Soon we will see those mountains," he promised.

Saul kept watch, and soon he saw a bit of greenness in the distance. The greenness grew larger. Now Saul could see trees on the mountain peaks. The vessel was skirting the coast of Lebanon.

"From those mountains came the cedar for the mast of our ship," the captain told Saul. "The oars are made of oak."

Saul's father nodded. He remembered a poem from the prophet Ezekiel about a city of Lebanon once famous for shipbuilding. He repeated the words aloud.

Raise a lamentation over Tyre, and say to
   Tyre,
      who dwells at the entrance to the sea,
      merchant of the peoples on many coast-
         lands,
   thus says the Lord God: ....
"Your borders are in the heart of the seas;
   your builders made perfect your beauty.
They made all your planks
   of fir trees from Senir;
they took a cedar from Lebanon
   to make a mast for you.
Of oaks of Bashan
   they made your oars;
they made your deck of pines
   from the coasts of Cyprus,
      inlaid with ivory. ....
all the ships of the sea with their mariners
   were in you, to barter for your wares." [11]

The captain shook his head.

"Tyre isn't so prosperous these days," he answered. "Caesarea is the Roman capital of this region."

"Jerusalem is the real capital," Saul wanted to say, but the ship was coming into the port of Caesarea now. He could see the sea wall and the two stone towers that guarded the entrance to the harbor. The water of the Mediterranean was so clear that he could see the huge chains which could be dropped from one tower to another to close the port to unwanted ships.

"The city was built by King Herod," Saul's father explained. "He named it in honor of Caesar Augustus. The palace of the Roman governor of Judea is here, though he has a residence in Jerusalem also. He is always in Jerusalem at Passover time, for he fears an uprising of the Jews."

The ship had docked now, and Saul and his father greeted their Jewish friends who had come to the port to meet them.

"We plan to start for Jerusalem in the morning," the Jewish friends told the two pilgrims from Tarsus.

6.
Passover Time

Still hearing the sound of the sea and smelling the fragrance of fresh springtime flowers, Saul slept that night in Caesarea. He was up when the sun rose the next morning, helping his father to refill the wineskins and pack a new supply of dried fish and fruit for the journey.

It was almost seventy miles to Jerusalem, and they would walk every step of the way. Some of the older men might ride. All of them would camp out at night.

Soon the caravan was ready to start. Jews from other parts of Cilicia, as well as from Cappadocia and Rome, from Greece, and even from North Africa had joined the pilgrims from Tarsus for the journey.

The caravan made its way down the streets of Caesarea, out of the city, and on through the hills south of the nearby mountain range. The pilgrims could see Mount Carmel as they camped for the first night.

Around the smoldering coals, an old man pointed to the highest peak and spoke of the ancient prophet Elijah who had dared challenge wicked King Ahab to a contest on Mount Carmel.

Saul knew the story well. He pretended that a bit of the dark green he had seen on a slope of the mountain was the very juniper tree under which Elijah

47

had mourned when he fled from the anger of the king.

"It was on that mountain that the angel of God brought the prophet a cake baked on hot stones and a fresh jar of water," Saul's father reminded him.

"Another prophet was once there too," Saul volunteered. "The woman from Shunem had to ride a long way and climb the mountain before she could find Elisha and ask him to come and help her sick little boy."

"These men know all of our history," Saul's father told his son. "It is not fitting that you should seem to instruct them."

Saul said no more, but he kept thinking about Mount Carmel and the stories his mother had told him of happenings there.

On the caravan went the next day, to the south and then east. On one side of the trail the pilgrims could see the bare, rocky slopes of Mount Gerizim, and on the other side, Mount Ebal.

"There, on Mount Gerizim, was once the temple of the Samaritans," Saul's father told him. And he spat in disgust.

"Why do we hate the Samaritans so?" Saul asked.

"They do not worship as we do," his father replied. "Every real Jew knows that Jerusalem is the place to worship." He paused.

"But what could be expected of a half-breed race like the Samaritans!"

Soon the pilgrims could see a clump of trees that marked the place of Jacob's well. Saul knew the story of Jacob's digging the well, but he listened to one of the men tell it again. Saul helped another man let down water jars and pull them up overflowing with fresh, cool water. Never had a drink tasted so good to him. He gave thanks for his ancestor Jacob who had dug the well and for the underground springs of water that flowed down from the mountains and filled it.

Now the caravan was passing through land which Joshua had once assigned to the tribe of Benjamin. Saul did not need his father's reminder that this was the country given long ago to the tribe to which he belonged.

His father pointed to the east. "Benjamin's land extended even to the banks of the Jordan River," he told Saul. "It reached south almost to the Dead Sea. In it there were rich fields and walled cities."

"Even the city of Jerusalem?" Saul asked.

"Benjamin's portion almost included Jerusalem," his father replied. "We are nearly to the city now. We shall walk through the gate of Benjamin into the city. One of the gates of the Temple is also named for our tribe."

Saul walked very straight and stood as tall as he could. He was still thinking of his great ancestor when he heard singing.

> I was glad when they said to me,
> "Let us go to the Lord's house!"
> And now we are here,
> standing inside the gates of Jerusalem! [12]

It was a psalm long used by Temple pilgrims on their way to Jerusalem.

His father pointed up the road. Saul looked and caught his breath.

There, surrounded by low-lying hills, was the city. Saul remembered a verse he had loved ever since his mother had taught it to him.

> As the mountains surround Jerusalem,
> so the Lord surrounds his people, from
> now on and forever.[13]

It was true! The mountains were on every side of the city, protecting it.

Saul could see Mount Zion. A bit of shining white marble gleamed in the sunshine. The Temple!

Saul's father pointed out a bit of the old wall which King David had first built around Jerusalem, and Nehemiah had rebuilt hundreds of years later. He showed his son the second wall and some of the city gates—the Sheep Gate and the Fish Gate. "There are twelve in all," he reminded Saul.

"What's that tall mass of stone?" Saul asked.

"That is the Tower of Antonia where the Roman soldiers have their headquarters," his father replied. "Near it is the palace where Herod lives when he is in Jerusalem."

Saul's eyes were looking toward the Temple. He could see the shining roof now, but there was no more time for talk.

The pilgrims had reached the gate of Benjamin and were entering the city.

The narrow streets of Jerusalem were crowded with merchants and pilgrims who had come from many countries, but Saul and his father finally found their way to the house of Jesse where Saul's father had often stayed during the Passover.

"I thought you would come," Jesse said as he welcomed the travelers. "I am glad you have brought your son. I remembered he was old enough and saved a bed for him."

It was late, and not until the next morning could Saul and his father go to the Temple.

They started early, for they must arrange for sacrifices and buy a lamb for the Passover meal.

"You will eat Passover with our family," Jesse reminded them.

Ever since he could remember, Saul had looked forward to being in Jerusalem at Passover time, but he had not thought of the jostling crowds that blocked the narrow streets and pushed a boy out of their way. Merchants shouted on every side to attract customers, and the sound of hooves clattered on the cobblestone streets. The air was heavy with the smell of sweat and animals and overripe figs and vegetables.

"It will be different in the Temple," Saul assured himself. He followed his father across the Brook Kidron and up the hill to the Temple gate. There they took off their sandals, for inside the ground had been declared holy. They entered the Temple court.

Saul almost drew back from the scene which met his eyes. On every side merchants had made stalls for the animals brought to sell for sacrifices. Saul could see the struggling sheep and the doves beating their wings against the wooden mesh of their cages. He could see the bearded moneychangers at their tables with coins piled high in front of them. He heard the bleating of lambs, the frightened cry of birds, and the shouts of the merchants and moneychangers.

Saul watched as his father bought a lamb and exchanged Roman coins for Jewish ones to pay for it. He saw the lamb killed. Then he and his father waited their turn to present the sacrifice.

As they waited, Saul saw a man with poor eyes buying a sheep. When the merchant realized that the man was almost blind, he took the fat sheep that the man had selected by feeling of it and slipped it back into its pen. Then he gave him a skinny ram instead.

When another man went to have his money changed into the coin of the Temple, Saul saw the moneychanger slip one of the Jewish coins from the correct change and put it into his pocket. Every buyer had to have his Roman coins changed into Jewish money, for Jewish rules required that the sacrificial animals be purchased with Jewish coins. There was an additional charge for the exchange of the Roman money which every pilgrim carried. Time and again Saul saw the merchants and moneychangers cheat their customers. He was glad when the trumpets of the Levites sounded, and he and his father could go with some others to offer their sacrifices.

The priests came into the Temple yard carrying gold and silver trays. They blessed the sacrifices which the people offered and indicated the part to be placed on the altar. There was more blowing of trumpets. When the ceremony was over, Saul and his father carried what was left of the slain lamb home with them.

They could already smell the smoke of the burning pomegranate wood over which the lamb would be roasted.

Wine and bitter herbs and unleavened bread were on the table with the lamb. At last the meal was ready.

The streets of Jerusalem were quiet now. Passover had begun.

As the youngest son present, Saul asked the old, old question first commanded in the ancient Law. "What do you mean by this service?"

"It is the sacrifice of the Lord's Passover," his father

replied, "for the angel of the Lord passed over the houses of the people of Israel in Egypt when he slew the Egyptians but spared our homes."

Saul did not need to be told that his ancestors had first observed that Passover the night before they left Egypt. He knew that the herbs represented the bitterness of their slavery and that the slain lamb represented sacrifice. He thought of the blood of the lamb on the doorposts of those long-ago homes in Egypt. All his life Saul was to remember his first taste of Passover food in Jerusalem and the sound of his father's voice as he explained what the service meant.

In the morning, the pilgrims went again to the Temple. As Saul and his father crossed the outer pavement and walked toward the marble steps which led to the inner court, Saul stopped in amazement. Before him on a slab of stone, he saw an inscription cut in bold Greek letters. It said:

LET NO FOREIGNER ENTER WITHIN THE SCREEN AND ENCLOSURE SURROUNDING THE SANCTU- ARY. WHOSOEVER IS TAKEN SO DOING WILL HIM- SELF BE THE CAUSE THAT DEATH OVERTAKETH HIM.

Saul knew what the word *foreigner* meant to a Jew. It meant a Gentile, any man who was not born a Jew or who had not become a Jew by the rite of circumcision. "If Apollonius were with me, he could not go inside," Saul thought to himself.

Perhaps his father read Saul's thoughts. "We Israelites are the only chosen people," he reminded his son. "Of course we are the only ones allowed in the inner court. Gentiles who come here must remain in the outer court with the women."

Inside the court of the men, Saul saw the fires still smoking on the altar. Before him and up more steps he could see the Holy Place in which he knew was the Holy of Holies. Saul stood for a long time looking up at the beautiful curtain which hid the Holy of Holies. His fingers longed to touch the material made of twisted linen threads, and his eyes feasted on the rich blue and scarlet and purple embroidery.

At last he turned and walked slowly back into the Temple court.

In one of the porches, he found a learned rabbi explaining the Scriptures. Among the listeners were several boys about Saul's age. They were actually asking questions, and the teachers were answering them.

Saul knew that men like this one would be his teachers. Perhaps he would ask them some of the questions in his mind. Would they take time to explain things to him?

For two weeks Saul and his father enjoyed the festival in Jerusalem. Then it was time for the pilgrims to leave.

Saul walked with his father down the narrow street that led to the gate of Benjamin. His father kissed him good-by, and Saul bent his head for his father's blessing.

The caravan passed through the gate.

Saul stood alone and watched until it was out of sight. Then he walked slowly back to the house of his father's friend where he would make his home while he went to school in Jerusalem.

DEUTERONOMY 13:8–10; MATTHEW 23:33; ACTS 3, 4

7.
A Young Pharisee

Saul's education in Jerusalem began at once. He was studying to be a teacher and a lawyer in the Jewish courts.

The Roman officials were the civil governing body in Palestine, the final authority which the people must obey. The hated Roman eagle even hung above the gate of the Temple, and the high priest himself was appointed by the Roman governor. Caiaphas, the present high priest, realized that he held office because of his political alignment, and he acted as an appeaser.

Yet the Romans did allow the Jewish people to have their own courts which decided matters relating to their religion. And the Jews had rules relating to practically everything in life.

In Jerusalem there were two Jewish schools for advanced study. Saul entered the school which had been founded by Rabbi Hillel years before.

There, as in the synagogue school in Tarsus, the center of study was the ancient Law, both written and oral.

The recorded Law had originally included the first five books of the Old Testament. To this Law of Moses had been added many rules and traditions of the elders and scribes, and few people distinguished between the two.

In Saul's school, there was no book of instruction except the Old Testament Scriptures, and all the teaching was given orally.

Saul was disappointed that there were no other textbooks. He had hoped for books on poetry and astronomy.

In Tarsus he had learned every rule given him, but he found that there were more and more prohibitions.

"You may tap the ground with your foot," one rule about the sabbath said, "but you must not rub your sandal along the earth. That would be plowing."

Saul learned that he must not gather even one stalk of wheat on the sabbath or rub the grains out of it, for that would make him guilty of harvesting. He must not light a fire.

He learned exactly how many steps he could take on the sabbath day. If he wished to go outside the city, he could evade the Law by going there the day before and depositing enough food for two meals. Such a place became his technical "home," and he was said to be only "going home."

Saul even learned one rule which told him exactly how he must stand when he said his prayers!

With the other students, he sat each day in a small group and listened to his teacher. Sometimes they were in a porch of the Temple and sometimes in a synagogue.

They listened first as the teacher read a passage from the Law in the Hebrew language. Then they listened as he translated the words into Aramaic, for all of his students had not had Saul's advantage of learning Hebrew.

When the reading was finished, the teacher began his explanation of the passage. He interpreted it by using allegories and the opinions of the ancient rabbis. He knew better than to offer a fresh comment, for men must think only in line with the old, accepted explanations.

Saul was delighted that the pupils were allowed, and even encouraged, to ask questions, but he was disappointed that most of the questions had to do with matters that were not important.

"Must we give a tenth of even the small garden herbs like mint?" one man asked.

The teacher replied, "Yes."

"How about tiny plants for seasoning, like cumin and anise?" another wanted to know.

Again the teacher said, "Yes."

There was little talk of truth and justice, and mercy was scarcely mentioned.

Saul especially liked one of his teachers, Gamaliel. He was a grandson of Hillel who had founded the school, and, like his grandfather, he loved the beauty and culture of the Greeks. Sometimes he spoke of these things. Even today that same Gamaliel is referred to as one of the most famous Jewish teachers of the first century.

Saul thought of Apollonius and the Greek teachers in the groves of the university in Tarsus. He smiled when Gamaliel quoted from Greek literature. Saul learned to depend on this teacher for honest answers.

Saul's father had been a Pharisee, and Saul too lined up with the Pharisees. He fiercely supported Jewish Law and the right of the lawyers or laymen rather than the priests to interpret it.

This attitude meant that Saul also believed in associating only with men who obeyed the same rules he did; especially must he not associate with a Gentile, a man who was not a Jew.

Saul loved to argue, and sometimes he argued with another student about the beliefs of the Pharisees and the Sadducees.

"There is no life after death just as the Sadducees say," one student argued. "There are no rewards or punishments."

As a Pharisee, Saul disagreed violently. And he usually won the argument.

Saul soon learned that the Sanhedrin was the highest court of the Jews. Especially important were its decisions in matters that had to do with the Law of Moses. Many of the seventy men who composed it were Pharisees.

The Sanhedrin met in a stone room in the Temple court.

One day Saul and a few other students were allowed to enter the room and observe its sessions. The case had to do with a man accused of blasphemy.

Saul learned that this court was allowed to pronounce the death sentence on such a man, but the sentence could not be executed without the approval of the Roman authority.

Saul listened to the fierce arguments between the Pharisees and the Sadducees. To his amazement, he saw them join forces against this man accused of breaking the Law of Moses. He saw them cast their votes and pronounce the death sentence for the crime of blasphemy.

Under his breath, Saul repeated the command against a man who broke the Law of the Sabbath or uttered blasphemy.

Neither shall thine eye pity him,
neither shalt thou spare, . . .
but thou shalt surely kill him; . . .
thou shalt stone him to death with stones.[14]

As he thought what a stoning would be like, Saul remembered his mother and some of the stories she had told him. Most of those stories he remembered had been about prophets. They had been kind and had helped people. Saul thought of a day when a young Greek boy had been wounded in a street in Tarsus. No Jew would touch him to give aid, but Saul had seen pity in his mother's eyes.

Somehow, as Saul remembered the flickering light of the sabbath candles and the sound of his mother's voice, he was homesick for her and for his father. He would walk to the Gate of Benjamin and remember the river in Tarsus.

Though he had no textbooks on astronomy or mathematics, Saul learned a bit about those subjects from oral instruction. He listened to men talk in the marketplaces, but his school was "the house of interpretation," and that interpretation was of Jewish Law—the Law of Moses plus the additions that had crept into it.

Saul studied in Jerusalem for several years. Then he probably went back to Tarsus and lived there for a time, making tents and teaching. He must have been there at the time of Jesus' ministry and visits to Jerusalem. Some historians think Saul married, for the rules of the Sanhedrin said that a member of that group must be married, and Saul later referred to voting in the Sanhedrin. Perhaps his wife died soon after the marriage, for there is no reference to her in his letters.

One day the young Pharisee went back to Jerusalem.

Familiar as he was with the bickering of the Pharisees and Sadducees, Saul was hardly prepared for the bitterness and violent hatred which he found in the Sanhedrin. Both Pharisees and Sadducees were talking about a sect which had grown up in Judea and Galilee while Saul was living in Tarsus. One of the Pharisees told him about it one day.

"A little more than three years ago," he explained, "a young Jewish carpenter began to travel about the country teaching and preaching, and, some say, healing diseases. His friends dared say that he even raised the dead to life."

"Ridiculous!" Saul almost snorted the word. Then he asked, "What was his name?"

"Jesus of Nazareth," replied his informer. "He became popular with so many people that we were losing our influence on the crowds. He had to be silenced. The man even claimed to be the son of Jehovah God!"

"That is blasphemy!" Saul almost shouted the words.

The man nodded. Then he said slowly, "He was crucified."

Saul stared in amazement. "A Jewish teacher crucified!"

"Yes," the Pharisee replied. "We worked it so that some of the people demanded it. The Sadducees agreed with us that the man was dangerous to our religion and to the Jewish nation. Death by crucifixion was demanded. The Romans let us have our way."

"Well," Saul waited a moment, "it's all over now."

"We thought so," the Pharisee said, "but his followers claim that he rose from the dead and walked among them for a time. They say that before he went back to God, he told them to spread his teachings and tell people about him.

"One day these followers of the Nazarene began preaching in the streets of Jerusalem, calling the man the Messiah whom God had promised the Jewish nation. Crowds sided with them, and the movement has grown ever since."

"It is a strange story," Saul said.

He asked the teacher Gamaliel about it one day.

"It is true," Gamaliel said. "Jesus of Nazareth often spoke in the Temple courts. He seemed a courteous and brave man, though a misguided one. If we had only been more cautious, the movement might have died. As it is . . ."

He paused for a moment and then went on.

"As it is, his followers are zealously teaching about him. Some of them are reported to be doing wonders among the people, healing the sick and crippled just as they say the man they call their Master did."

"The stories couldn't be true," Saul said. "Have you yourself seen any of these followers of the man from Nazareth?"

"Yes," Gamaliel answered, "the Sadducees brought two of them before the Sanhedrin, charging them with preaching that their leader had actually risen from the dead. As you know, nothing irritates the Sadducees like the mention of resurrection."

"What kind of men were the two arrested?" Saul questioned. "Had they been trained in the Law here in Jerusalem?"

"No," Gamaliel replied. "They were fishermen from

Galilee. The strange thing was that there came with
them that old lame beggar who used to sit at the gate
of the Temple. He actually walked into the courtroom."

"Walked!" Saul exclaimed. "He has never walked
since I came to Jerusalem."

Gamaliel nodded. "His parents say he had never
taken even one step since the day he was born, and
that was forty years ago. Yet I saw him standing there,
claiming that the two fishermen had healed him in the
name of Jesus of Nazareth."

"What did the court do?" Saul inquired.

"What could they do?" Gamaliel asked. "There
stood the man as strong and straight as you or I, and
the people who had followed him into court were
shouting that God had healed him."

"The court had to do something, didn't it?" Saul
asked.

"The court ordered the two men—Peter and John
were their names—not even to speak the name of
Jesus again."

Gamaliel was quiet for a moment. Then he added
slowly, "You'll have to say one thing for those two
fishermen even if they were not educated in the Law.
The court couldn't scare them. What do you suppose
they said?"

Saul shook his head. "I can't imagine two ignorant
fishermen daring to say anything to the Sanhedrin."

Gamaliel almost smiled. "Those two fishermen
stood their ground. They said firmly, 'We cannot keep
quiet about our Lord. We must tell the things we have
seen him do and heard him say. We must obey God
rather than men.'

"All the onlookers were shouting and praising God

for the lame man's healing. The court dared not punish the prisoners. The judge only blustered and threatened them if they continued to talk about Jesus. Then he released them."

"It's a strange story," Saul said. "I would never have believed it if you yourself had not told me."

He thought for a moment.

"Are all the followers of Jesus of Nazareth uncouth and ignorant people like these fishermen?" he asked.

"No," Gamaliel admitted. "Barnabas, of Cyprus, is an educated man and a wealthy one. He is known for his openmindedness and generosity, but he's not too good a speaker."

He waited a moment.

"Go on," Saul urged. "Is he the only one?"

Gamaliel shook his head.

"There's a man named Stephen . . . ."

Again he paused.

"What about Stephen?" Saul asked.

"It is late now," Gamaliel said. "We'll talk about Stephen another time."

8.
What about Stephen?

Saul could not forget Gamaliel's story about the lame man who had been healed. What had happened? he wondered. Could Gamaliel have been mistaken? As a Pharisee, Saul did not consider the two fishermen important, but Gamaliel, his teacher, was different. And Gamaliel claimed that he had actually seen the lame beggar walking as well as any man.

Saul decided to find out for himself. If he gave the beggar a piece of money, perhaps he would tell him the truth and reveal the trick. For Saul was sure that there was a trick somewhere.

Early one morning Saul made his way to the Temple. At the gate called Beautiful, where the lame man had sat for so many years, he stopped, for he saw a beggar. But this was a young man, only a boy, and he was not lame. He was standing on two feet, holding out his hand for money and pointing to his blind eyes.

Saul stared in amazement.

"Where is the lame man?" he asked.

The boy shrugged his shoulders.

"I'm blind," he said. "How should I know? He comes here no more. My friends tell me that he has a job and walks with not even a limp. I don't know. But this is a good spot for beggars, and it's mine."

"Where does the man live?" Saul asked.

"I don't know," the boy replied. "I'm just glad I have his place here at the Temple gate."

Saul asked several people about the man, but no one could give him any information.

"He really wasn't important," Saul decided. "He must have been an ignorant man, and his story wouldn't have been worth much."

Then Saul thought of the man Gamaliel had mentioned last. Gamaliel had seemed to think that Stephen was different. He had promised to tell Saul about him.

Opportunity came one day in the Temple porch when the last student had gone home, and Gamaliel sat alone.

Saul went to him.

"My teacher," he said, "what about Stephen?"

Gamaliel did not answer at once. Then he put his hand on Saul's arm.

"Sit here with me, my son," he invited. "I will tell you all that I know about Stephen."

Saul sat down, and together the two watched the setting sun.

"I heard of Stephen only a few weeks ago," Gamaliel began. "He is a member of the group of people who follow the teachings of Jesus. They call themselves 'followers of the Way' or the church. The group includes Jewish people born here in Palestine and some born in Greece. Few of them are rich, and all of them share what they have with those who need food or clothing. There are many widows in the church, and some of the members suspected that the widows of Grecian Jews were not getting the help they needed. Since the leaders didn't have time to investigate every case, the church chose seven men to help them in distributing food and clothes—*deacons* they call them.

"Stephen was one of the men chosen to be a deacon. He is a Grecian Jew and has a good reputation for wisdom and integrity. The followers of the Nazarene say that he is full of the spirit of helpfulness and joy as their Master was.

"This Stephen did not stop with ministering to the poor and seeing that each widow got her rightful share. He was always helping people, and, some say, he was doing miracles of healing just as the two fishermen did."

"Is that all?" Saul asked, a bit disappointed.

"Not quite," Gamaliel said. "This Stephen even went into one of the synagogues and began to argue with the assembled Jews about Jesus of Nazareth. He spoke so well that some of the Jewish priests were convinced. They believed on Jesus as the Christ and joined the group of his followers. This so incensed the leaders of the Sanhedrin that they decided Stephen's mouth must be stopped. There is a rumor that witnesses have been found who declare that they heard the man speak blasphemy. Whether or not this is true, I do not know, but Stephen has been arrested."

"May the blasphemer get what he deserves!" Saul exclaimed.

Gamaliel did not reply for a moment. Then he said, "Sometimes I do not know about these followers of the Nazarene. Stephen's case comes up before the Sanhedrin tomorrow. You, Saul, will be there to see Stephen and hear for yourself what he says."

The next day dawned bright and clear in Jerusalem.

As Saul dressed, he remembered that this was the day for Stephen's heresy trial. He thought of the trial he had once witnessed as a student. He remembered the verdict of the court—death by stoning. In his mind Saul could almost hear the voice of his fellow students as he had repeated with them the ancient command regarding a man found guilty of blasphemy.

> Neither shall thine eye pity him,
> neither shalt thou spare, . . .
> but thou shalt surely kill him; . . .
> thou shalt stone him to death with stones.[15]

Saul brought his mind back to the present. Carefully he went through the ceremonial washings of his hands. He repeated his morning prayers as any devout Pharisee would do. Then he walked briskly to the stone room in the Temple area where the Sanhedrin met.

The Pharisees and Sadducees were not bickering today. All of them seemed intent on the young man who was on trial.

The judge opened court and asked, "What is the charge against the man Stephen?"

Saul leaned forward to hear the witnesses.

"He is always talking against our ancient Law and the ceremonies of the Temple," they said. "We have even heard him say that this Jesus of Nazareth whom he follows will someday destroy the Temple and change the customs which Moses taught in the Law."

The crowd growled and turned to look at the prisoner.

Saul turned too and almost started from his seat in amazement. He saw before him not an uncouth foreigner, but a man of culture and poise whose face glowed with a light that reminded Saul of the steady shining of the lamp that burned before the Holy Place in the Temple.

The judge was speaking to the prisoner now.

"Is the charge true?" he asked.

Saul waited for the denial that he was sure would

come. Of course this man would deny such blasphemy.

The prisoner began to speak, and Saul and all the court listened.

They heard Stephen tell of God's call to Abraham and of his care of the Jewish people and nation from the days of Moses to the days of King Solomon.

If Stephen had stopped then, he might have gone free, for every Jew believed in the dealings of God with their people. But Stephen did not stop with recounting Jewish history.

"Solomon built a great Temple for the worship of the Lord God," he said. "Yet God does not dwell in a temple made by the hands of men.

"You men are resisting God's Spirit today just as your fathers did long ago when they killed the prophets. For you have murdered Jesus, the Christ whom God sent."

Mutterings grew into rumblings, and rumblings became shouts. Sadducees and Pharisees gnashed their teeth at the accused man.

Saul drew back from their fury and looked at the prisoner who seemed not to be noticing the angry men holding his very life in their hands.

Stephen was looking up, and he seemed to see beyond the stone walls that housed the court. His lips moved, and Saul, with all the Council of the Sanhedrin, heard his whispered words:

"I see him!"

Stephen's voice grew louder, and his face was shining with a great light. Even the onlookers heard what he said.

"I see the heavens opening and Jesus standing at the right hand of God!"

The members of the Sanhedrin clapped their hands over their ears to shut out the words.

"Blasphemy!" they shouted, and they rushed at the prisoner and dragged him outside the city. There was no thought of waiting for Roman sanction.

Saul followed the mob to the place of stoning. There he stopped.

"Stay here and take care of our coats," an older man ordered him.

Saul saw both Sadducees and Pharisees throw aside their outer robes and leave them at his feet. He watched as they took up sharp stones and began to hurl them at their prisoner.

Saul's eyes followed the stones, and he saw that Stephen's face was still shining like light. He was looking up.

As Saul stood quite still, he heard Stephen's words, "Lord Jesus, receive my spirit."

He saw Stephen kneel as if before a mighty king, and he heard his whispered prayer, "Lord, do not hold this sin against them."

The jagged stones did their cruel work. Stephen fell to the ground, and when Saul looked at his face, he seemed asleep.

The members of the Sanhedrin brushed the dust from their hands. They picked up their coats from Saul's feet and walked away.

Saul looked at Stephen's bleeding body and thought of the Law's command against a blasphemer, "Neither shall your eye pity him."

Suddenly Saul felt sick.

9.
I've Made up My Mind

In Jerusalem both the Pharisees and Sadducees were jubilant.

"After what we did to Stephen, those followers of the Way won't dare mention Jesus of Nazareth again," one of them boasted.

"What Way?" inquired a bystander.

"It's something about the teachings of their leader," a Sadducee replied. "Those fellows declare that it is more important to live by the Way of love that Jesus taught than it is to obey the Law itself. What happened to Stephen should stop such nonsense and talk."

The Sanhedrin waited to see what would come next. They knew Rome did not like mobs. Would the government blame them for the disturbance at the time of Stephen's death? More important, had their act really stopped the preaching about Jesus?

Especially when he was alone, Saul was thinking. He considered all that had taken place in the city since the followers of Jesus began preaching that God had raised him from the dead.

Three thousand people had declared their faith in Jesus on one day. They had joined the group of believers in him.

Saul knew that the number was now reported to be more than five thousand and that the church included some of the priests of the Temple.

Instead of stopping the disciples, the imprisonment of Peter and John had only added to the talk about the healing of the lame man in the name of Jesus of Nazareth.

"Threats and beatings seem to have little effect on these believers," Saul told the Sanhedrin one day. "We must see that this talk about Jesus is stopped."

An old man shook his head.

"Is that still going on?" he asked. "What are they saying now?"

"The same thing," Saul replied. "They never stop talking about Jesus of Nazareth. They blame us for his death. I myself heard them say that God raised Jesus from the dead and that it is the power of their living Lord which enables them to do wonders. They even say . . ."

Saul paused a moment, and the group leaned forward to hear what he would tell them.

"Go on," they urged.

"Those people even say that Jesus of Nazareth was the long awaited Savior of our nation whom God promised through the prophets and that there is no other way for even the best of us to be saved except by believing on him and following his teachings."

"Blasphemy!" The scribes and Pharisees shouted the word together.

"Let Saul decide what we must do," someone suggested.

In his own mind Saul had already decided.

"God has given us the Law of Moses," he declared firmly. "At all costs, we must see that it is obeyed. That Law says that a man guilty of blasphemy must die."

And in his heart Saul thought, There is no truth to

these stories about Jesus' power. Maybe if I prove my loyalty to God by stamping out this heresy, I can forget Stephen's face.

"I'll fix those blasphemers," he said aloud.

The members of the Sanhedrin gave their approval. With a zeal that surprised even himself, Saul began personally to hunt out followers of the Way.

On every street he entered house after house and tricked suspected believers into declaring their faith. Then he dragged them away to be beaten and imprisoned.

Wives wept as they saw their husbands seized and dragged off. Helpless men in chains hid their eyes from the sight of their wives being herded to prison like cattle to a pen. Little children hid themselves in dark corners and cried for their mothers and fathers.

Some of the believers fled from the city, but many of them had no place to go. Many had no money to use for traveling or making new homes.

The prisons in Jerusalem were crowded with believers in Jesus Christ.

And still those followers of the Way would not keep quiet.

"Today I heard a man tell his brother of the crucifixion and resurrection of Jesus," one informer said.

"I heard a mother tell her little girl of a promise Jesus made to his disciples," another chimed in. "She even repeated the promise, 'Lo, I am with you always.' "

"Even the boys and girls are talking nonsense about the man from Nazareth."

"Aren't these people afraid?" someone asked.

"Of course they are," the informer replied. "Who wouldn't be afraid after what happened to Stephen?

They run from Saul of Tarsus like rabbits from a hound. But they do not stop talking. Tales about Jesus and his power continue to spread."

One day rumors came that there were believers in the city of Samaria.

"That is where Philip went when he fled from Jerusalem," a man explained. "He has been preaching about Jesus in Samaria just as he did here in Jerusalem. Many Jews there are believing what he says and are joining the church."

Another day someone reported that even as far away as Damascus, in Syria, the Jews were not only hearing about Jesus, they were actually becoming believers.

Saul decided that something must be done to stop the spread of such heresy. He went to the high priest.

"I've made up my mind that these followers of the Way must be wiped out," he announced. "This preaching about Jesus of Nazareth must be stopped at any cost. We must get rid of these believers in other cities as well as here in Jerusalem."

The high priest agreed.

"What is your plan?" he asked Saul.

"Let's start with Damascus," Saul suggested. "You have influence there, and the Jewish community is ruled by Jewish law. Give me a letter to the synagogues of the Jews in Damascus. Tell them to cooperate with me in arresting every man in the city who even speaks of Jesus of Nazareth. I will bring those blasphemers here to Jerusalem for trial, and we can deal with them. We must make an example of every person who dares break the Law of Moses."

The high priest looked at Saul with interest. The plan might work, he thought. It would be a feather in his cap if it did, and the Sanhedrin would be rid of those stubborn believers who were making so much trouble.

The letter was written, and Saul carried it home with him.

Before he went to sleep that night, Saul sat for a long time on the rooftop. He repeated the evening prayers of a good Pharisee.

As he looked up at the shining stars, once again he remembered the light on Stephen's face. Would the believers in Damascus look like Stephen, he wondered.

Early next morning, with some of the Temple guards, Saul set out on his journey. Damascus was more than a hundred miles to the north, and Saul was anxious to get there and begin his search for believers.

As he passed through the Jerusalem gate, Saul carried the high priest's letter in his pocket. In his heart he carried a fierce determination to stamp out faith in Jesus Christ.

10.
I Saw Him

The road from Jerusalem to Damascus was paved with huge stones since Roman soldiers often galloped over it. Caravans of merchants traveled it also, for Damascus was a center of trade and in Jerusalem were buyers of embroideries and silks and spices. Saul and his companions met both soldiers and caravans of commerce.

Impatiently Saul urged his companions to more speed, but no camel, mule, or donkey could be persuaded to travel very fast in the hot sun that beamed down on that stony road to Damascus. Saul resigned himself to a trip of perhaps two weeks.

Yet he was still restless. At night, while his companions slept, Saul sat staring into the darkness.

There was so much to think about. The road they were following led through country famous in Jewish history. Saul was thoroughly familiar with that history.

One night he and his companions camped by the side of a well that Jacob had dug near the city of Sychar, in Samaria. Saul drew water from the well, enough for his beasts as well as for himself and his companions.

He recalled that he had seen that well years before when he was a boy. He also remembered that God had spoken to Jacob. He knew that it had been many years since any man of Israel had dared say he heard the voice of God.

Farther on, the road led through the Plain of Esdraelon, and Saul thought of David and his small army that had once encamped there when they were fighting the Philistines.

"Look far away at those hills!" one of the men with Saul exclaimed as they crossed the plain. "How near they seem! We can almost see the town of Nazareth which lies beyond them."

"Nazareth!" Saul almost spat out the word. The name reminded him of the growing number of people who had decided to follow Jesus' Way rather than the way of Jewish Law.

"Nazareth is accursed because of the man Jesus," he muttered.

He was still seething with anger when the blue Sea of Galilee came into view.

Saul remembered that in dozens of little villages along the shore, people were still talking about the mighty works Jesus of Nazareth had done in their towns.

The road led through Capernaum, a thriving center for fishermen.

As Saul rode through the streets, he recalled that this city had been headquarters for Jesus and his disciples. Here crowds had thronged about him, bringing sick and lame people to be healed. In the synagogue, Jesus had even dared break the law which forbade healing on the sabbath day.

Saul was glad when Capernaum and the Sea of Galilee were behind him and out of sight. There was a straight road north into Syria from this point.

"We will reach the city soon," he announced.

The journey continued.

Each night as Saul and his companions stopped to rest, Saul felt in his pocket to be sure that the letter the high priest had given him was safe. The believers in Damascus must soon pay for their disloyalty to the Law of Moses. In his mind he reviewed his plans for their extermination.

"Getting rid of those heretics is a part of my service to God," he assured himself.

As they approached Damascus, Saul and his companions rose even earlier than usual. They put as many miles as possible behind them before the heat of the day. It had been a hard journey, and they were tired. The road was dusty, and it would be good to reach the city and bathe in cool water.

On one day the morning had almost passed when one of the guards gave a shout.

"Look," he exclaimed, "far in the distance, a spot of greenness."

"It is Damascus," announced another who had traveled the road before.

Saul turned his head and stopped to look, but his eyes saw no greenness.

Instead, he saw a blazing light.

For a moment he thought of the light which had shone on Stephen's face, but it had been nothing as compared with the light he was now seeing. This one was brighter than the sun at noonday.

Saul and his companions fell to the ground, and Saul heard a voice speaking to him in the familiar Hebrew language which he had learned in childhood.

"Saul, Saul, why are you persecuting me?"

Saul thought of the believers in Jerusalem whom he had imprisoned, and of Stephen, to whose death he had consented.

"Who are you, Lord?" Saul stammered.

"I am Jesus of Nazareth whom you are persecuting," the voice replied. "It is hard for you to kick against the pricks."

"What shall I do, Lord?" Saul asked.

His companions stared at him, for they had heard no voice.

But again Saul was hearing it.

"Rise and go into Damascus, and there it will be told you what you are to do. Stand on your feet, for I have appeared to you that you may preach about me to the Gentiles, that they too may have forgiveness and faith."

Slowly Saul rose from the ground. His companions saw him reach out to touch them, and they realized that he could not see. They took his trembling hand.

"Judas who lives on the street that runs straight through the city will receive us," they told each other.

As Saul groped his way up the road and on through the gate into Damascus, he spoke only once. His companions leading him were near enough to hear his whisper.

"I saw him!" Saul said. "I saw the Lord Jesus!"

II.
The New Believer in Damascus

In Damascus Saul's companions led him down the street called Straight to the house of Judas. Then they went their way, for there was much to see. Damascus was the oldest city in the world, and it was famous for the bazaars that lined many of the streets.

Alone, Saul waited. He wondered what he must do. He could not see or sleep. He was not hungry, but question after question pounded in his active mind. His whole way of living and thinking was upset—his profession as a defender of Jewish Law, his habits as a Pharisee, his family training, his idea of God and what he wanted a man to do.

Most of all, his idea of Jesus of Nazareth had completely changed.

Saul knew now that Jesus was no imposter. His followers who claimed that he had risen from the dead were telling the truth. Saul had seen him!

He had heard him speak, and he knew with certainty that God approved of Jesus of Nazareth. He knew that there was something higher than the Law, and that something was Someone—Jesus the Christ whom the Jews had crucified and whom God had raised from the dead.

Saul also knew something else. In fighting the believers of the Way, he had been fighting against God himself!

Now God had called him—Saul of Tarsus—to preach the gospel of Jesus Christ to the Gentiles. How must he begin?

For three days Saul pondered his experience and what it meant, and as he pondered, he prayed. It was as he prayed that in his mind he saw a man coming to him and restoring sight to his blind eyes.

Saul waited.

As he sat alone the third day, he heard a knock.

"Enter," he called, "I am blind and cannot see to open the door."

Saul heard the door open. Then his ears caught the sound of strange footsteps.

"Who are you?" Saul asked.

Saul felt a steady hand on his arm and heard a deep, gentle voice.

"Brother Saul," a man assured him, "I am a believer in the Lord Jesus Christ. My name is Ananias.

"The Lord Jesus, who appeared to you on the road to this city, has sent me that your eyes may be healed and you may be filled with his Holy Spirit. Receive your sight."

Saul lifted his eyes, and once more he could see!

"You must have something to eat," Ananias said. "You need your strength."

So Saul ate.

Afterwards, he told Ananias his experience on the road to Damascus.

Ananias nodded his head.

"I understand," he said.

"Has the Lord spoken to you also?" Saul asked.

Ananias smiled.

"The Lord called me by name," he said.

"He told me to get up and come immediately to this house and inquire for you.

"I was amazed, for I had heard about you and how much evil you had done to the believers in Jerusalem. I knew that you had come here with authority to arrest every follower of the Lord Jesus.

"The Lord was very patient with me," Ananias continued. "He told me that you were praying and that he had chosen you for a special work, to preach the gospel of Jesus Christ to Gentiles and Jews and kings."

"What must I do now that I too am a believer in the Lord Jesus?" Saul asked.

"Let us seek other followers of the Way," Ananias suggested. "You are a believer, and you must be baptized."

Saul agreed, and Ananias took him to a room where the followers of Jesus were meeting. They could hardly believe their ears when Ananias introduced Saul as a believer, for they, too, knew why he had come to Damascus.

Yet they trusted Ananias, and they could not long doubt Saul's sincerity. Soon he was baptized and became a part of the fellowship of the church in Damascus.

Immediately Saul began preaching in the synagogues of the Jews.

"We Jews were mistaken about Jesus of Nazareth," Saul told his hearers. "He is the Christ, the Son of God."

His listeners were amazed.

"Is not this the man who led the persecution of the church in Jerusalem?" they asked. "Did he not come here with authority to arrest and rid the city of believers in Jesus?"

Saul had destroyed the letter from the high priest in Jerusalem. Now he needed to be alone to make some plans.

How could he tell his father that he had found something higher and better than the Law of Moses and had become a follower of Jesus? How could he preach the gospel to the Gentiles? Were they, after all, as important to God as his own people, the Jews? How did God want him to begin the new work? What would be his message?

These and other questions crowded into Saul's mind. And he reached one conclusion. He must be alone and think things out.

One day he slipped away from his friends and left Damascus.

Years later he mentioned that solitary time in one of his letters.

> I did not go to anyone for advice, nor did I go to Jerusalem to see those who were apostles before me. Instead, I went at once to Arabia, and then I returned to Damascus.[16]

Back in Damascus, Saul once more began his preaching to the Jews.

"Jesus is the Christ," he declared, and he proved his point by recounting Jewish history.

Many of the Jews were converted to the Lord Jesus. They joined the church.

Jewish leaders in Damascus became uneasy. As the Sanhedrin had done in Jerusalem, they decided to get rid of the man they held responsible for disturbing the people.

"We will have to kill this renegade," they decided. "Get the king to have guards posted at the gates of the city. They must watch day and night so that Saul of Tarsus cannot escape alive."

Saul and the other believers heard of the plot.

One night, several believers crept quietly through the darkness to a house built in the city wall. They carried a large basket, and with them was Saul of Tarsus.

"The owner who lives here is a follower of the Way," someone assured Saul.

A man opened the door. Motioning for silence, he led Saul and his companions to an upstairs room and pointed to a high window.

"It opens above the wall," he whispered.

His visitors nodded, for every step of the plan had been discussed the day before. They placed the basket near the window, and Saul stepped into it and crouched as low as he could.

His friends tied a stout rope to the basket and lifted it to the window. Carefully they pushed it through the opening. Then, very slowly they let out the rope.

Saul was out of the basket as soon as it touched the ground. His keen ears could hear the footsteps of the guards at the nearby gate.

For several moments, Saul stood in the shadows close against the wall. When he could no longer hear the guards' footsteps, he set out for Jerusalem.

12.
Will They Understand?

"I must see Peter and find out more about Jesus!"

Over and over, the resolve pounded in Saul's mind as he headed south for Jerusalem. Sometimes the thoughts were so powerful that he spoke aloud.

"Peter was one of the men who went about the country with Jesus for more than two years. From him I can learn much about Jesus and his teachings."

Along with the desire to hear more about his Lord, Saul had a question that was almost a fear: Will they understand?

"Will the believers whom I persecuted in Jerusalem understand that I am really a changed man and am now a follower of the Lord Jesus? Will my old friends in the Sanhedrin understand that I, who once led the persecution of believers, am now convinced that God raised Jesus of Nazareth from the dead? Can I make them see that he is indeed the Christ whom God promised?"

Saul of Tarsus went over all these questions in his mind as he traveled the long miles from Damascus to the Jewish capital city.

What would he do when he got to Jerusalem? The Sanhedrin would call him a turncoat, a traitor to the Law. Would the believers think him a spy?

Saul flinched when he thought of those believers. Some of them were men and women whom he had put in prison three years before. Some were families of men for whose death he had been responsible. How could he convince them that he had a changed purpose in life, that he wanted to serve the Lord Jesus as they did? Would any man trust him? Certainly not the high priest whose letter to the Damascus synagogues Saul had destroyed. Certainly not James, the leader of the church he had persecuted.

Who would help him when he got to Jerusalem? As Saul wondered about that, he thought of Gamaliel's remark that two of the believers seemed more open-minded and different. If only Stephen were alive, he might understand. Although he came from Greece, he knew Jewish history and what the Law could mean to a man.

Saul shook his head. There was no use thinking of Stephen, and it reminded him of the place of stoning.

At last Saul remembered that Gamaliel had mentioned another man. He had spoken of Barnabas as a kind person, a Jew from the island of Cyprus. Maybe Barnabas would have a more open mind than the Jerusalem Jews. He, too, was a believer. Maybe he would take Saul's word that he had become a follower of the Way.

Slowly the miles slipped by. Minutes stretched into hours, and hours lengthened into days, for Saul was traveling on foot. There had been no time or opportunity to arrange for transportation.

Yet the long journey never altered Saul's fierce determination. "I must learn all I can about Jesus. I must convince people that these believers are right about him. Will they understand that Jesus is the Christ and that I am his follower?"

At last Jerusalem came in sight. As Saul walked

through the gate into the city, he saw Herod's palace. He also saw the Temple where he had so often worshiped God. He remembered the stone room where the Sanhedrin met, and he knew that there both Pharisees and Sadducees were united in their determination to get rid of faith in the Lord Jesus Christ.

Saul wondered how he could find Peter. He decided that the best way was to visit the believers.

It was not hard to learn where they were accustomed to meeting, and there Saul made his way.

As he opened the door of the room, he saw a small group of men and women. They started at the sight of a stranger. Who was he? What did he want?

They looked at him questioningly, and Saul spoke.

"I am Saul of Tarsus," he said.

Saul saw the men and women draw back with horror in their eyes, but he went on.

"I come to you as a believer in Jesus Christ. I have been wrong, dreadfully wrong."

Still the believers stared at the man who stood before them. They said not one word, but slowly, one by one, they slipped out of the room—all but one man.

When the two were alone, the man came close to Saul and held out his hand.

"My name is Barnabas," he said. "Are you really a believer in the Lord Jesus Christ?"

"I am," Saul replied, and he told Barnabas how Jesus had spoken to him on the road to Damascus. He told about his call to preach to the Gentiles and about speaking in the synagogues in Damascus and how the Jews there had plotted to kill him.

"I especially want to see Peter," Saul explained. "I want him to tell me all that he knows about Jesus."

"I will take you to him," Barnabas promised, "but tonight I want you to come with me to another meeting of these same believers."

Saul shook his head at the thought of facing those unfriendly eyes again. Could he do it?

Barnabas put his hand on his arm, and Saul agreed.

That night the two men made their way to another meeting.

The believers were startled when they saw that Saul was with Barnabas, but Barnabas held up his hand.

"I know that this man is Saul of Tarsus who once persecuted us," he said, "but I trust him. Listen to his story."

Saul did not deny that he had indeed persecuted the followers of the Way. He told of his planned trip to Damascus and how Jesus had appeared to him and called him to preach to the Gentiles. He told of speaking in the synagogues in Damascus and of the Jews' plan to kill him.

His listeners relaxed a bit. They knew what it meant to be persecuted. They recognized that Saul spoke with sincerity and was really one of them, a believer in the Lord Jesus Christ.

When the meeting was over, they were his friends, and they took him to Peter's house.

For fifteen days Saul stayed in Jerusalem. Peter told him about the Lord's Supper and the appearances of Jesus after the resurrection. He spoke of the earlier days when he and the other eleven disciples had gone about the country with their Master. And Saul listened carefully to every word.

When he was not talking with Peter, Saul was preaching. In the synagogues he argued with the Jews

that Jesus was indeed the Christ promised of God—
the Redeemer. Some of the Jews listened to him and
became believers. Others were enraged.

Jewish leaders began to hate Saul with a fierceness
that matched the feelings he had had when he set
out to exterminate believers.

"This man Saul must be destroyed," leaders of the
Jews decided, and they plotted to kill him.

Some of the believers heard of the plot. They
begged Saul to leave the city, but he would not agree.
He wanted so much to convince his old friends that
he was sincere, and he longed for them to share his
faith in his Lord.

Finally the believers led Saul to see that for his
work for Christ to continue, he must leave Jerusalem.
At last he realized they were right.

"It might be well for you to go to Tarsus," they
suggested.

Saul agreed.

The next day, some of his friends accompanied
him out of Jerusalem and on to the coast, to the city
of Caesarea by the sea. There Saul boarded a boat for
Tarsus.

He must have remembered his first sea trip with
his father and the long talks they had. He thought
of his family and sighed.

"Will they understand?" he asked.

Saul never revealed the painful scene which must
have taken place when he reached Tarsus and told
his family of his new faith. Neither did he speak of
his old friends among the Grecian people who lived
there. Only one thing did he mention. In one of his
letters, he wrote:

It was three years later that I went to Jeru-

salem to get information from Peter, and I
stayed with him for two weeks. . . .

Afterward I went to places in Syria and
Cilicia. At that time the members of the Christian churches in Judea did not know me personally. They knew only what others said,
"The man who used to persecute us is now
preaching the faith that he once tried to destroy!" And so they praised God because of
me.[17]

Because Tarsus was the largest city in Cilicia, Saul
made his headquarters there, and there Barnabas
found him when he came from Jerusalem one day.

Delighted as he was to see his old friend, Saul
sensed that there was a special reason for the visit.

"Why are you here in Tarsus?" he asked.

"Many things have taken place since you left Jerusalem," Barnabas replied. "As you know, the believers
who were scattered abroad at the persecution of
Stephen never ceased to witness to their Lord."

"I know," Saul said, and there was sadness in his
voice. He still blamed himself for that persecution.

"Go on," he said.

"Everywhere they went, those believing Jews
preached to other Jews. Some of the believers who
fled to Antioch in Syria had been born in Cyprus and
Cyrene. They knew the Greek language, for they had
had Grecian neighbors in the country of their birth.
These men did not limit their preaching to the Jews.
Antioch is full of Grecian people, and those believers
began preaching to Greeks as well as to Jews.

"A great number of those Grecian people believed
on the Lord Jesus.

"News that Gentiles were being received into the

church in Antioch came to the church in Jerusalem, and I was sent to Antioch to investigate."

"What did you find?" Saul asked.

Barnabas smiled.

"I found that God was working with those Gentiles," he said. "Many of them were believing on our Lord.

"The church in Antioch is growing," Barnabas continued. "It needs a good preacher."

Barnabas looked straight at his friend.

"Saul," he said, "Saul, we need you to preach to the church at Antioch."

It did not take Saul long to make up his mind what to do.

His Lord had told him he was to be an apostle to the Gentiles, he reasoned. These believers in Antioch were Gentiles. This must be the work to which God had called him.

Soon Saul and Barnabas were on their way to Antioch, the capital of Syria.

13.
The Church at Antioch

"Tell me more about Antioch." Saul made the request as he and Barnabas traveled the road which wound through the Taurus Mountains to the plains and on toward Antioch in Syria.

Barnabas hesitated.

"I have heard that it is an evil city," Saul went on. "I hear that even in the name of religion, unspeakable and immoral deeds are done."

Slowly Barnabas nodded his head.

"Yes," he admitted, "there is much wickedness in Antioch. It is a large city. Many of the people there worship heathen gods in the groves on a nearby hill.

"As you know, Antioch is the Roman capital of Syria, but even the Roman governor is shocked by what goes on in those groves. He has made it a penal offense for one of his soldiers even to visit the place."

"All this wickedness in the name of their gods!" Saul was thinking aloud. "Have these people no idea of the one great God, the Lord who is righteous and commands that his people live by righteous standards?"

"I doubt that most of them have ever thought of such a god," Barnabas replied. "You can understand how much there is to teach those who have become believers in the Lord Jesus Christ."

"Are all the people in Antioch Gentiles?" Saul asked.

"Most of them are," Barnabas replied, "but there is a colony of Jews. Antioch offers these merchants free citizenship which is not available in many places. "Grecians and many other Gentiles have found peace in the love of our Lord. They make up the church, and they are eager to learn more about Jesus and his way of living."

When the two men reached Antioch, they saw a busy city with wide streets and beautiful buildings. Its location reminded Saul a bit of Tarsus, for ships sailed up the Orontes River from the Mediterranean just as they had sailed up the Cydnus to Tarsus.

Yet Saul's chief interest was not in the river or its commerce. It was in the church at Antioch. It had no building and no equipment, but it had the one real necessity for a church—devoted believers in the Lord Jesus Christ, believers who were eager to learn his Way of living and to have fellowship with God.

News that Barnabas had returned spread throughout the city.

"Barnabas will be at the meeting tonight," believers told one another. "He has brought a stranger to Antioch with him."

That night, Saul of Tarsus again faced a group of people, some of whom mistrusted him. They knew he had persecuted the believers in Jerusalem. Some of them had even been forced to leave their homes because of him.

Yet these believers trusted Barnabas more than they doubted Saul. They listened to what Barnabas told them about Saul's preaching the gospel for more than a dozen years, even in the face of threats.

They listened as Saul himself told of meeting Jesus on the road to Damascus and of his call to preach the gospel. When he spoke of Jesus, they heard a tone in his voice and saw a light on his face which no one could doubt.

The church at Antioch accepted Saul, not only as a brother in their fellowship but as one of their teachers.

For more than a year Saul and Barnabas worked together, helping the church at Antioch to understand what it really meant to follow the Lord Jesus Christ.

More and more people joined the group of believers.

These believers were quick to change their evil ways and to follow Jesus' Way of right and love.

So zealous were they that the people of Antioch gave them a nickname.

"They are always talking about one they call Christ," the people said. "They even try to act like him!"

And the people in Antioch began to call the believers "Christians."

These Christians soon had another opportunity to show Jesus' spirit of love and helpfulness, for news came that there would be a great famine, especially in Judea.

The Christians in Antioch did not hesitate. They brought gifts—"every man according to his ability."

"Take this money to the believers in Judea," they directed. "They will need food."

Barnabas and Saul set out for Jerusalem. They would take the money there and let the church distribute it.

When they arrived in Jerusalem, they delivered the gift and asked for news of the church there.

"We are sad here in Jerusalem," one of the believers reported. "Herod Agrippa, king of Palestine, ordered James put to death with a sword."

"Not James, the pastor of the church here?" Saul interrupted.

"No," explained the man, "James, the brother of John. He was a follower of our Lord, you remember. When the king saw how much this evil act pleased the Jewish leaders, he had Peter arrested."

"Is Peter in prison?" Saul asked.

The man smiled a bit as he went on with his story. "Peter was put in prison," he said. "All we could do was to pray for him. This we did, and the Lord opened the prison doors and delivered him."

"Is Peter still preaching?" Saul asked.

"Yes," the man answered. "Strict Jew that he is, he even went into the home of Cornelius, a Roman commander, and told him about the Lord Jesus and his Way of forgiveness and fellowship with God. The Roman and some of his friends believed in our Lord, and God gave them his Spirit just as he has given it to Jewish believers in Jerusalem."

"What did the church in Jerusalem say about Peter's disregard of Jewish rules?" Saul asked.

"They questioned Peter," the man admitted. "Peter explained that God had directed him to preach to the Roman. He said:

" 'God seeks men of every nation. He has granted unto Gentiles as well as Jews the gift of life in Jesus Christ. He gives his Spirit to all who really believe in him.' "

"Peter too is preaching to the Gentiles," Saul told himself. "God is speaking through him to men of other nations just as he is speaking through me. He wants all peoples to come into fellowship with him through faith in the Lord Jesus."

The conversion of Cornelius was much in Saul's

mind as he and Barnabas returned to Antioch. With them, they took young John Mark, a nephew of Barnabas.

In the church at Antioch, God was teaching the people not only through Barnabas and Saul but through other leaders. There was Simeon Niger whose Latin name *Niger* means "black." There was Lucius from Cyrene, a Greek city in North Africa, and Manaen who had been brought up with Herod Antipas at the king's court.

One day as Barnabas and Saul and these other teachers fasted and prayed together, God's Spirit put into their hearts and minds a new work to do.

"Set apart for me Saul and Barnabas for the special work to which I have called them," the Holy Spirit directed.

Saul knew what that work was. God had called him to it years before. He was to go to faraway places and preach the gospel of Jesus Christ to the Gentiles.

The teachers told the church at Antioch what God's Spirit had directed.

Together the Christians fasted and prayed that they might indeed know and obey the will of God.

They did not argue that many people in their own city had not heard the gospel. They did not mention their own preferences that the two men remain with their church. They did not beg Barnabas and Saul to stay with them.

Instead, the members of the church at Antioch in Syria asked God's special care for these two teachers whom they loved so much. Then they laid their hands on the heads of Saul and Barnabas in blessing and sent them away.

That night Barnabas and Saul left the city. With them went young John Mark of Jerusalem.

14.
On the Island of Cyprus

West of Antioch, about sixteen miles away, the Orontes River widened, and five miles from its mouth stood the city of Seleucia. Barnabas and Saul and John Mark set out for Seleucia.

"God has called us to preach to the Gentiles," Barnabas and Saul told each other. "We must go into Gentile country. We must leave the east coast of the Mediterranean, for that is the home of the Jews."

"We will probably find some Jews wherever we go," Saul remarked.

Barnabas agreed. "That should help us in our preaching," he said, "for the heathen may at least have heard of the one Lord God."

"Where shall we go first?" Saul asked.

The three men prayed about that, and Barnabas suggested the island of Cyprus.

"That is my old home," he reminded his companions. "I grew up there, and I would like my countrymen to hear the gospel."

"Some of the believers went there when persecution forced them to leave Jerusalem," John Mark volunteered. "I hear that they have been preaching to the Jews on the island."

"Are there many Jews on Cyprus?" Saul asked.

"Some have invested in the copper mines there," Barnabas answered him. "There are several synagogues on the island."

"Do you suppose anyone has preached the gospel to the Greeks and the native Cypriotes?" Saul asked.

"I doubt it," Barnabas answered.

The city of Seleucia was in sight now, and the three men made their way to the river. The Orontes was deep here, and ships from Cyprus were constantly sailing the five miles up from the Mediterranean Sea.

As Barnabas, Saul, and John Mark neared the water, they saw the dock piled high with fruit, copper ore, bales of flax, and other freight.

They could see that Seleucia had an excellent port with flood gates from the inner to the outer harbor. Looking down through the clear water, they could see the great stones of the piers.

"Those stones are twenty feet long," Barnabas said, and he pointed out the iron clamps which held them together.

It was not hard to find a ship bound for Cyprus, and Barnabas, Saul, and John Mark boarded one.

As the ship sailed down the river, the three looked back at the stony hills which rose like a fortress behind the city. Soon the hills were dim in the distance, and the travelers turned to face the open sea.

It was a clear day, and far away they could see a tiny speck on the horizon.

"What is it?" Saul asked.

"That is the island of Cyprus," John Mark and his uncle Barnabas answered together.

"How large is it?" Saul asked.

Barnabas smiled. "You always want to know the size of things, don't you, Saul? Cyprus is not very large, but it has two good ports. The eastern port is Salamis where we will dock. It has been a Roman city for a hundred years now. Before that time, it was ruled by the Assyrians, the Egyptians, the Persians, and the Greeks. Some say it is so old that it must have been settled by the Phoenicians."

"Such a place will have many heathen superstitions," Saul said.

"Yes," Barnabas agreed. "The people in Cyprus are gullible and superstitious. They need to know the true God and his Son Jesus Christ."

It was a sail of only a few hours to the island, for Cyprus was just sixty miles off the coast of Syria.

Soon Barnabas pointed out the bit of land shaped like a fist with the forefinger pointing eastward. Both he and John Mark were familiar with the island, but its orchards and forests were new to Saul.

As they approached the dock at Salamis, Saul immediately recognized the signs of trade and commerce. He noted the lumber and copper ore. Farther on he could see some of the buildings. He pointed out one.

"That house looks like a synagogue," he said.

"There are a number of synagogues in Salamis," Barnabas replied. "We will go to all of them."

"We will preach in the synagogues first," Saul agreed, "but we must not stop there. Our orders are to preach to the Gentiles."

The ship had docked now, and the three missionaries soon stood on the island of Cyprus.

As they had planned, they went first to the synagogues of Salamis and preached to the Jews there about the Lord Jesus. Then they made their way across the island to the Roman capital of Paphos.

And as they passed through the small towns, they preached there too.

The road was good, and soon the three men reached
Paphos on the western side of the island. Once long
ago, Paphos had been a Phoenician settlement, but
now it was Roman with a population made up largely
of Greeks.

The residence of the Roman governor was the center of the city's life.

"The present governor is Sergius Paulus," Barnabas
told Saul. "He is an intelligent Roman, and some say
he no longer worships idols. Yet he is superstitious
and has an astrologer at his court. The astrologer in-
fluences him a great deal. He is a Jew who calls himself Elymas, and he thinks of himself as 'the wise.' "

Saul thought about the situation. Should he tell the
governor that he was a freeborn Roman citizen? He
decided to introduce himself by his Roman name, and
from this time on, he was spoken of, not as Saul, but
as Paul.

When the governor of Cyprus heard of the three
strangers in his city who were preaching about the
one Lord God, he sent for them to come to the palace.

"Tell me about this religion you preach," he
ordered.

Paul introduced himself and began to tell Sergius
Paulus about the one true God and his Son Jesus
Christ. He told of the forgiveness and peace which
faith in the Lord Jesus can bring.

As he spoke, the governor leaned forward to listen,
and Paul saw that he was deeply interested.

The astrologer Elymas was standing by. He, too,
saw the governor's interest. He frowned. Then he
began to interrupt, and to argue, and to do everything
he could to belittle Paul's message and draw the
governor's attention away from it.

Paul saw that the astrologer's antics might keep the governor from understanding the gospel. He knew he must do something.

Suddenly he turned to Elymas and spoke sternly.

"You are a slick rascal," he said, "a deceitful trickster. You are an enemy of honest thinking and right living. Will you stop trying to twist the gospel of Jesus Christ?"

Elymas only sneered.

Paul looked him straight in the eyes.

"God will stop your evil work," he said. "For a few days you will be blind, not able to see even the light of the sun."

Elymas staggered back. He tried to brush the mist from his eyes, but it was no use. He stretched out his hands, and a court attendant led him away.

The governor watched in amazement.

Now he could give full attention to what Paul was saying.

"The one true God raised Jesus from the dead," Paul continued. "Through faith in the Lord Jesus, there is forgiveness and fellowship with God for every man."

The governor was astonished at such teaching.

"You must be preaching the true religion," he said slowly.

Because of what he had seen and what he had heard, the Roman governor believed in the Lord Jesus Christ.

Paul's foreign mission work had begun. In a Roman city in Cyprus, he had preached the gospel of the Son of God, and a Gentile had believed. From now on Paul would be known as the Apostle to the Gentiles.

15.
To Their Main Job

As Paul and Barnabas stood at the port of Paphos on the island of Cyprus and looked toward the northwest, they faced the coastal country of Pamphylia.*

Pamphylia was new territory to Paul, and he liked to explore new places. Yet he wanted to go into Asia for another reason. There were people there, and most of them were not Jews. They were Gentiles.

Paul and Barnabas thought of those people as they planned to leave Cyprus.

"God wants them to hear the gospel of Jesus Christ just as he wants all people to hear it," they declared. "Preaching to them is a part of our mission to the Gentiles."

Thus Paul, Barnabas, and John Mark found a small ship and set sail for Perga, a town in Pamphylia.

The trip was short, for the mainland was not far away. Soon Paul and his friends saw a long, coastal plain with tall mountain peaks behind it.

When the ship docked and the men faced toward the town, the cool breeze from the sea changed to a hot wind from the land. Summer was beginning, and the heat grew more unbearable as the three made their way to Perga.

---

* Author's note: Pamphylia was located north of the eastern end of the Mediterranean. It was a part of the country now known as Turkey. Paul would not have known the name *Turkey*. When he was preaching, this whole area between the Mediterranean and the Black Sea was called Asia. That Asia of the first century A.D. was divided into several smaller countries, one of which was Pamphylia.

While the men were at Perga, John Mark decided to return to Jerusalem. Paul and Barnabas faced all the possible difficulties in their way, and yet they knew they must go on.

"To the north is Pisidia," a man told them. "There you will find a large city named Antioch."

"Another Antioch!"

Paul and Barnabas repeated the words together as they looked at each other and smiled.

"Yes," the man responded. "If you want to go there, you had better find a caravan you can travel with. The road is rough and dangerous. It is infested with robbers, and pirates hide in rocks. Sometimes a flash flood sweeps down from the hills, and a caravan is washed away."

Paul and Barnabas thought longingly of the broad road that led into Antioch in Syria, but they did not change their minds.

"We will go on," they said, and they followed one of the caravans out of the city.

The road led through the lowlands into barren country, on and on, through narrow paths with high cliffs on each side.

Often, in a broader spot, the travelers saw great patches of salt and sometimes a lake of salt water.

Soon Paul and Barnabas could see rugged mountains. As they climbed the peaks, they found less and less grass and fewer and fewer trees.

Yet the air was cooler, and the two men breathed it gratefully.

Years later Paul was to remember that rugged country and write in one of his letters that he had been "in perils of waters, in perils of robbers."

Some of the caravans camped in the hills, but Paul and Barnabas climbed higher and higher. When they were more than three thousand feet above sea level, they found that the road opened out into a wide plain, and in the distance, they saw a city—Antioch in Pisidia.

As they came nearer, they could see the aqueducts and forts which the Romans had built. They could even see the Roman eagle over the gate of the city. They would find that this was indeed a Roman city. Even the money had Latin words on it.

Paul and Barnabas were glad to learn that this Roman city had a synagogue, and there they went to worship on the sabbath day.

It was especially good, in this heathen city, to join in the opening words of the service which began, "The Lord our God is one God."

Paul and Barnabas joined in the prayers too. They listened to the reading of the Law and of the prophets.

The leader of the synagogue saw the two strangers. When the reading was finished, as was the custom, the leader invited them to speak.

"Brethren," he said, "if you have any word of encouragement for our people, say it."

Paul stood up. Before him he saw not only Jewish people but also Gentiles who had once been heathens but had learned to honor the one true God. He beckoned for all the people to listen to him.

"Hear me," he began.

First, he reminded the Jews of God's care of their nation and spoke of the greatness of King David.

The Jews nodded their approval. They were not prepared for his next statement.

"Of this man's posterity God has brought to Israel a Savior, Jesus, as he promised."

Paul had gotten to the heart of his sermon now. He was preaching about the Lord Jesus.

"Our Jewish people in Jerusalem did not recognize this Savior," he explained. "Neither did their leaders. They condemned him and asked that he be killed. Jesus was crucified and buried."

Paul paused for a moment. Then he said, "God raised Jesus from the dead!"

The people stared at him. They leaned forward to listen more closely as he continued to tell of men and women who saw Jesus after the resurrection.

"We bring you the good news that God has kept his promise of a Savior," he went on. "Through faith in Jesus Christ, there is forgiveness of sin and freedom from burdens which the Law can never bring."

Freedom! Something more powerful than the Law of Moses!! These people had never even dreamed of such a thing.

When the meeting was over, they crowded around Paul.

"Tell us more about this Jesus next sabbath," they begged.

And some of them, both Jews and Gentiles, followed Paul and Barnabas out of the synagogue.

"Continue to learn of the grace of God," Paul advised them. And he taught them during the week.

All over Antioch, people were hearing the good news about Jesus. On the next sabbath day, both Jews and Gentiles crowded the synagogue.

Again Paul spoke to them, but this time the leaders of the synagogue disputed what he said.

"Jesus was an impostor," they declared.

Paul and Barnabas knew what they must do. Sadly they faced these men who represented their own people. Slowly, but boldly, they answered them.

"We felt that you should be the first to hear the good news from God. By turning away from it, you

have proved yourself unworthy of the eternal life
which Jesus makes possible."

The two missionaries pointed to the men and
women who were not Jews.

"Behold, we turn to the Gentiles," they announced.
"The Lord has commanded us just as one of our
prophets said long ago:

'I have set you to be a light for the Gentiles,
That you may bring salvation to the uttermost
     parts of the earth.' " [18]

Now the astonished Gentiles were staring at Paul.
Soon their amazement changed to joy. They began to
praise God for the Lord Jesus, and many of them
believed on him.

The news spread to other Gentiles, both in Antioch
and in nearby towns.

Inside the city, Jewish leaders stirred up prominent men and women to get rid of Paul and Barnabas,
and the two were driven out.

From Antioch in Pisidia, the Royal Roman Road,
which began at Ephesus, led east across the plains.

Down that road, Barnabas and Paul made their
way. Their heads were high. They knew they were
doing the job God had given them, and he was blessing their work.

The two missionaries thought of the happy faces
of men and women who had believed in Jesus Christ,
and in their hearts were great joy and a sense of the
presence of their Lord.

"It is true," Barnabas whispered with awe in his
voice, "the promise Jesus' disciples told us about:

'Lo, I am with you always.' " [19]

16.
Plots in Two Cities

It was a busy road which Paul and Barnabas traveled as they left the city of Antioch in Pisidia, for it was the highway which the Roman government had built to carry soldiers from west to east.

The two missionaries met Roman soldiers returning from guard duty. They passed shepherds with large flocks of sheep and caravans of wool merchants with heavily loaded camels that often stopped to nibble prickly cactuses and tufts of salt by the roadside.

On across the plains, Paul and Barnabas made their way toward the city of Iconium.

The last part of the journey was on a road not so smooth or so wide, and the two men were glad when they saw an oasis in the distance. Its greenness rested their eyes, and as they came closer, they saw fields of flax and orchards of plum and apricot trees. They could even see a river flowing down from the mountains behind the city. They had reached Iconium.

As the two missionaries made their way through the marketplace piled high with flax and wool, they came to the building which Paul always sought first in any city—the synagogue of the Jews. They found the room crowded with both Jews and Gentiles, for in addition to its Jewish colony, Iconium included Greeks and natives as well as a few Roman officials.

111

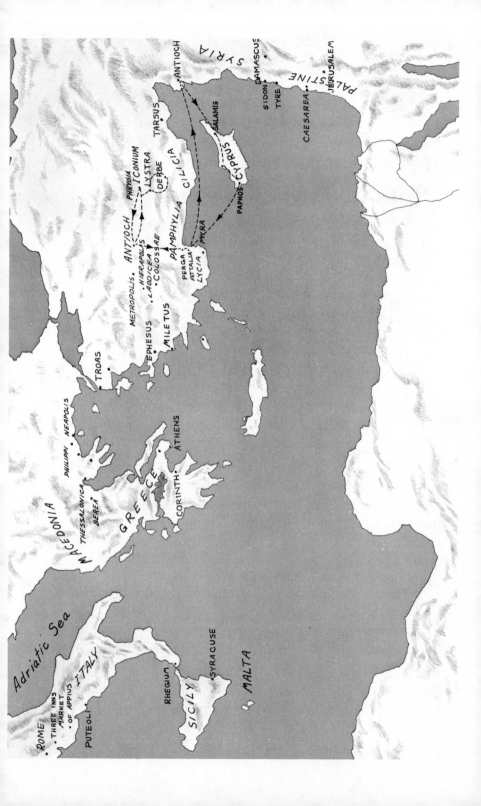

After the worship service, Paul and Barnabas received the usual invitation to speak. Barnabas nodded to his companion, and Paul rose to his feet.

So well did he preach the gospel of Jesus Christ that a great company of both Jews and Gentiles believed in the Savior.

And not only did the missionaries preach. Through the power of God, they were able to perform miracles and wonders in the city, and more and more people believed in the Lord Jesus.

These events enraged the Jews who did not believe the gospel. They began to poison the minds of the people against Paul and Barnabas.

One part of the city sided with the unbelieving Jews, another part with the two missionaries.

At last, enemies of the gospel plotted to stone Paul and Barnabas. They might have succeeded, but the two men found out about the plot.

It was time to leave Iconium, they decided, and they fled from the city on the road which led south toward Lystra.

It was a dreary road, so dry that in some places Paul and Barnabas saw travelers buying water from peddlers who carried it in skin bags slung across the backs of their camels.

When Lystra came into sight, Paul and Barnabas saw a Roman garrison. Soon they realized that they had come to the end of the Royal Road.

As they entered the city, the two men noticed an impressive stone temple dedicated to an ancient Greek god, Zeus, whom the Romans called Jupiter. They saw white-robed priests preparing oxen for a sacrifice to the god.

A soldier told them about the temple.

"There is an old story that someday Jupiter himself will return to the city with his messenger, Mercury, whom the Greeks call Hermes," he said.

Unlike other towns which Paul and Barnabas had visited, Lystra had few Jewish people and no synagogue. How would the missionaries begin their work?

As people gathered in small groups in the marketplace, Paul and Barnabas spoke to them in the Greek language, preaching about the Lord who alone is God.

A special opportunity for service presented itself one day when Paul saw a crippled man watching him and listening intently to what he was saying. There was a look of faith in the man's eyes from which Paul could not turn away, though he had been told that the man had never walked a step since birth.

Paul must have remembered how God had honored the faith of two of Jesus' disciples and had healed a lame beggar at the Temple gate in Jerusalem.

Suddenly he stopped his sermon. In his heart he prayed as he faced the crippled man and called to him, "Stand up on your feet!"

Immediately the man rose to his feet and actually began walking!

The crowd went wild.

"The gods have come down to us in human form!" they shouted. And they called Barnabas "Jupiter" and Paul "Mercury" because Paul was doing most of the talking.

The astonished preachers tried to explain, but the crowd was too busy talking. They pointed toward the temple of Jupiter.

The missionaries looked too.

They saw a white-robed priest leading out oxen with garlands hanging from their necks.

"We will sacrifice to these gods," the priest told

the people. And he pointed to Paul and Barnabas.

A procession formed.

The two preachers were horrified.

"Do nothing like this," they begged the people. "We are only men as you are. We have come to bring you good news that you must turn from your make-believe gods to the living God who made the earth and the sea and all that is in them. He has allowed all nations to choose their own ways, but he has never ceased to give you good things. This living God has sent you rain from heaven and fruitful seasons. He has gladdened your hearts with food and rich blessings."

It was hard to get the procession to turn back, but at last Paul and Barnabas succeeded.

And they kept on preaching whenever and wherever the people would listen to them.

One of Paul's most attentive listeners may have been Timothy. He probably was from Lystra and became a believer.

One day Paul noticed that the crowd was not as attentive as usual.

"I hear that unbelieving Jews from Antioch in Pisidia and from Iconium have come here and are making trouble for us," Barnabas told him that night. "They are telling the people that we are impostors. The people of Lystra are quick to listen to gossip, and some of them are spreading tales about us."

As Paul was preaching the next afternoon, he saw unfriendly faces in the crowd. However, he paid little attention until someone tossed a stone in his direction.

It was the signal agreed upon. A mob began to hurl rocks at the preacher.

The stones reached their target, and Paul fell to

the ground. The mob dragged him outside the city and, thinking him dead, left him.

Paul's friends heard of the stoning. They slipped outside the city to care for his body.

As they came near the spot, Paul lifted his hand. His friends ran to him. They brought cool water and bathed his face. Soon he could accompany them back into the city.

The next day the two missionaries left for the town of Derbe. There, too, they preached the gospel, and many people believed in the Lord Jesus.

"It is time to return to Syria," Barnabas said one day.

Paul agreed.

The two men set out over the same route by which they had come on their journey. They stopped at Lystra and Iconium, at Antioch in Pisidia, at Perga, and all the other towns where they had preached.

In each place, they encouraged the believers and begged them to continue strong in their faith in the Lord Jesus.

"It is not easy to follow the Christian Way," they reminded them.

In all the new churches, the missionaries assisted the Christians in choosing leaders to teach and help them.

They fasted and prayed, and commended the new believers to God's strengthening care. Then they said good-by and traveled on to the sea.

When they reached the Mediterranean, Paul and Barnabas boarded a ship at the port of Attalia. Soon they were sailing toward Antioch in Syria.

The first missionary journey was ending.

17.
What Would the Church Say?

News that Paul and Barnabas had returned from their trip spread quickly among the Christians of Antioch in Syria.

"Those are the two men God directed our church to choose for the work of preaching to the Gentiles," an old member explained to a new one. "They went out from us months ago on their journey. Now they have come home. I hear they have had strange adventures."

That night believers from all over the city hurried to a meeting of the church.

When the songs and prayers ended, the missionaries spoke.

Barnabas told of their stay in Cyprus and of the conversion of the Roman governor there.

Paul continued with an account of the work in Pisidia and the conversion of both Jews and Gentiles in that country.

Barnabas spoke of Paul's eloquent sermons and of his courage in time of persecution. He told of the work in the heathen city of Lystra and of the mob which stoned Paul there. Perhaps he mentioned young Timothy who had listened to Paul and had become a believer in the Lord Jesus.

Both men told of new Christians and new churches.

"Those Gentile believers in the Lord Jesus Christ

are really seeking to live his Way of rich fellowship with God and with each other," they reported.

As the Christians in Antioch heard how God had indeed opened the door of faith to the Gentiles, they rejoiced at the work Paul and Barnabas had done. Though the two missionaries tried to rest, they never refrained from telling of the many ways God had blessed them.

One day, as the Christians met together, Paul saw little groups whispering before the service began. The people seemed puzzled.

"What are you troubled about?" Paul asked.

No one answered for a moment.

"Some Jews from the church in Jerusalem are in town," a Greek Christian explained hesitantly. "These men say that God will not accept any Gentile unless he is first circumcised and becomes a Jew."

"We will talk with these men," Paul and Barnabas promised.

The men from Jerusalem were present at a special meeting one day, and Paul and Barnabas did talk with them. Over and over they argued the question.

"God has honored the faith of both Jew and Gentile," Paul declared. "He saves any man who believes in the Lord Jesus Christ."

The visitors from Jerusalem shook their heads.

"Impossible!" they shouted. "Salvation belongs only to the Jews."

The church at Antioch decided that something must be done. They appointed Paul and Barnabas and several other members to go to Jerusalem to talk over the question with the church there.

What would the church in Jerusalem say a Gentile must do in order to come into saving fellowship with

God? The Christians at Antioch wondered about that.

The delegates set out for Jerusalem. This time they took the road which wound through Phoenicia and Samaria. In every town where they stopped, Barnabas and Paul told of Gentiles who had been converted on their missionary journey.

The Christians were delighted and thanked God for his blessings on the work of the two missionaries.

In Jerusalem the church welcomed the group from Antioch. Again Paul and Barnabas told of the work God had done through them, saving and giving his Spirit to both Jews and Gentiles.

Many of the Jerusalem Christians rejoiced, but some who had been Pharisees could not see that the grace of God is bigger than the Law of Moses.

"These Gentile believers are not saved," they argued. "God will not accept them until they are circumcised and keep every Law of Moses. How can a Gentile be saved unless he first obeys the Jewish law of circumcision which came through Moses?"

"What a man cannot see with physical eyes is more important to God than that which he can see," Paul explained.

"God values most the faith that is in a man's heart. He does not judge him by what has been done to his body."

There was a long discussion.

Peter had been listening intently to all that was said. He had been remembering Jesus' command to preach the gospel to all people. Jesus had not even mentioned circumcision or other Jewish rules. Now Peter stood up.

"How can a Gentile be saved?" he asked.

Then he answered his own question.

He reminded the group that he, too, had preached to the Gentiles.

"God responded to the faith of those Gentiles," he declared. "He made no distinction between them and Jews who believed in the Lord Jesus. He gave them his Holy Spirit just as he has given that Spirit to us."

Peter looked the troublemakers straight in the eyes.

"You know that not one of us Jews has been able to keep all the Laws of Moses," he said. "Yet we believe that we shall be saved through the grace of the Lord Jesus, just as those Gentiles are. All men are saved in the same way."

Peter sat down.

Again Paul spoke.

"God worked signs and wonders with those Gentiles," he declared.

James, the pastor of the Jerusalem church, had been listening too. Now he spoke. He called attention to the words of an old prophecy which referred to Gentiles "called by the name of the Lord."

"It is my judgment that we should not trouble believing Gentiles with unimportant Jewish rules," he said.

"Let's write them a letter asking them, in their daily living, to avoid two or three practices that are especially offensive to Jewish people. They know these rules of eating and of moral living, for they are read in every synagogue."

James' solution seemed a good one, and the Christians in Jerusalem gave the delegates from Antioch a friendly handshake.

Carefully one of the members of the church in Jerusalem wrote out what had been decided. He wrote on parchment with a brush, making accurate letters.

When the ink was dry, the letter was read aloud to the church.

Most of the Jerusalem Christians were pleased with what it said. The letter was rolled up and wrapped in linen cloth, and Paul carefully put it into his pocket.

The next day Barnabas and Paul and the Antioch Christians returned home. With them went Judas and Silas to represent the Jerusalem church.

The members of the church in Antioch met together. They listened as the letter from Jerusalem was read. They rejoiced at the friendly words and good advice. Judas and Silas were introduced, and then they spoke. It was a time of good fellowship.

"We have been taught the truth," the Christians of Antioch assured themselves. "Gentiles can be saved in the same way Jews can be saved. The church at Jerusalem says there is only one way of salvation. A man must believe in the Lord Jesus Christ whom God raised from the dead."

Paul smiled.

"It is God who determines the way of salvation," he said. "The church has decided to free itself from the burden of the Law and preach the good news of salvation to all people through faith in the Lord Jesus. That is its message."

18.
New Workers

Winter was over in Syria. Red and yellow flowers were blooming, and bits of green showed through the melting snow on the lower slopes of the mountains. It was springtime.

Paul looked at those mountains and knew that the roads across them would soon be open for travel.

As he saw the young preachers in Antioch, he rejoiced in their growth and usefulness to the church. He was proud of their ability to preach the gospel.

Yet, as he watched them, there was in Paul's heart an ache which grew worse and worse. He was remembering the new churches in Lystra and Derbe and the other towns he and Barnabas had visited on their journey to the west.

Those churches had no trained teachers to help them. And there were still many, many people who had not yet even heard the gospel of the Lord Jesus.

One day Paul talked with Barnabas about what they should do.

"Let us return and visit the believers in every city where we preached the gospel of our Lord," he suggested.

"That is a good idea," Barnabas agreed. "I am sure John Mark will go with us."

"John Mark!" Paul was astonished. "Mark deserted us at Perga," he reminded Barnabas.

Barnabas defended Mark, and the two missionaries had an argument.

"I think Mark should go," Barnabas insisted. "Suppose I take him with me and go to the island of Cyprus. You can visit the towns on the mainland."

Paul agreed, and soon Barnabas and John Mark sailed for Cyprus.

"Who will go with me?" Paul wondered. "I need a companion."

One day he thought of Silas who had come to Antioch as a representative of the Christians in Jerusalem. He spoke to him about it.

"Would you like to go with me on a missionary trip?" he asked.

Silas hesitated.

"How could I help?" he asked.

"You know the gospel of our Lord," Paul declared. "Then, too, the old question of receiving Gentiles into the church is sure to come up. You will be especially helpful in speaking for the Christians in Jerusalem."

Silas was interested.

"I have a Roman name, too, just as you have," he told Paul. "It is Silvanus."

"That may be helpful as we preach to the Romans," Paul commented.

Silas agreed to go, and the church approved Paul's choice of a companion. Soon the two set out.

Going north and west, by the land route, they stopped at little churches in Syria and Cilicia.

"Welcome back, Paul," was the greeting in every church.

Paul introduced Silas, and both men spent some time teaching the new Christians and helping them with their problems.

"We must go on," they told the brethren one day. "There are so many other churches that need our help."

The Christians understood. They said good-by, and Paul and Silas went on to Derbe and Lystra.

Even before they reached Lystra, Paul heard good news of a young convert there.

"Do you remember Timothy?" someone asked him.

"Indeed I do," Paul said. "He believed in the Lord Jesus as I was preaching one day."

"He has a fine mother, too, and a good grandmother," the man reported. "They are Jews and have taught Timothy of the one true God. Both of them are Christians also."

"How about his father?" Paul asked.

"Timothy's father was a Greek," the man replied, "but he made no objection to teaching Timothy about the one true God. You will rejoice in the way Timothy has grown as a Christian."

Paul was very encouraged. He knew how much the new churches needed teachers with knowledge of God and his workings with men and women. He thought of Gentiles in many places who had never even heard of God's love or of the Lord Jesus. It would take many men to do all the work that was needed.

In Lystra, the church people gave Paul and Silas a warm welcome. Perhaps they wanted to help him forget the stones that had bruised him in their city.

"What about the young man Timothy?" Paul asked.

"He has helped us very much," the men of Lystra said. "He knows the Scriptures, and he lives by their teaching. He is a fine person and a good witness to our Lord."

Paul watched Timothy for several weeks. One day he talked with him.

"How would you like to go on a preaching trip with me?" Paul asked.

Young Timothy gasped in amazement. Paul was his hero, but he had never even dreamed of an invitation like this.

"It will be a good opportunity to tell people about our Lord Jesus," Paul explained. "The new churches especially need preachers who know the Scriptures. They need teachers to help them learn how God wants them to live every day."

Timothy thought about what Paul said. He thought of those new Christians and of the men and women who had never heard of the Lord Jesus. He talked the matter over with his mother and his grandmother, and all three prayed for God's guidance in deciding what Timothy should do.

"I will go with you," he told Paul one day.

Two missionaries had come to Lystra. Three made up the party leaving the city.

Across the Taurus Mountains, Paul, Silas, and Timothy made their way. It was a new road to Silas and Timothy, and Paul was glad to point out the tall peaks and tell of the journey he and Barnabas had made through this part of the country. He missed Barnabas, but he was too proud to say so. In his heart he realized that perhaps he had not been patient enough with young John Mark.

There was little time for Paul to brood about his argument with Barnabas, for there were many towns with new churches in them. And in all of these places, the missionaries stopped. Jewish troublemakers had been annoying them, and the churches were especially relieved to know that the Jerusalem Christians had advised them to have no hesitancy in receiving Gentile members.

Silas and Timothy were introduced. Both of them, along with Paul, preached in the cities, and more and more people believed in the Lord Jesus each day.

The missionaries could not spend much time in any one town. On through Phrygia and Galatia they went, planning a trip northward.

Yet, as they prayed about the matter, they came to feel that God's Spirit was not leading them in that direction, but toward the city of Troas, on the coast of the Aegean Sea.

The three men made their way westward to Troas.

"Will we preach in Troas?" young Timothy asked.

Both Paul and Silas shook their heads.

"We do not know just where God wants us to go at this time," they admitted. "Now we only know that we must go to Troas."

As the three men approached Troas, they saw a large city served by massive aqueducts which the Romans had built.

"It is the chief city and port of the province of Mysia," Paul explained.

Inside the city, he pointed out the marble Roman baths and the theater. He and his companions climbed the hill to see the temple built to honor the god Jupiter.

"These heathen certainly need the gospel," Silas observed, and the two other missionaries agreed. Yet none of the three knew how they should begin their work. They decided to think about it and look around the city.

The cool breeze from the ocean was strong in their faces as they made their way to the docks.

As they looked out over the blue water, in their

minds they could see the distant coast. To the south in Greece was the Roman province of Achaia, and to the north was Macedonia. There were Macedonians in Troas, and the missionaries could recognize them by their wide-brimmed hats and long coats cut in the style of the Greeks.

The missionaries again prayed for guidance in their work. But when they went to sleep that night, they had reached no decision as to where they would preach next.

That night Paul had a vision. In his mind, he saw a man standing on the faraway shore of Macedonia, and he heard a voice begging him to do something.

"Come over into Macedonia and help us," the voice said.

The next morning Paul told his companions that God was directing them to preach the gospel in Macedonia.

"We must leave Troas at once," he said.

It was in Troas that Paul met Luke, a physician. Paul found the doctor interested not only in medicine but in art and music and many other subjects that Paul had heard of in his childhood.

"I am a Greek," Luke told Paul, and Paul told him of his plan to preach the gospel in Macedonia. The trip appealed to Luke, and so did the Jewish missionary who felt he must preach to the Gentiles.

Soon another man had decided to go to Macedonia, Luke, whom Paul was later to call "the beloved physician."

The next day four men made their way to the docks at Troas.

19.
A Woman in Philippi

It was early when the little ship left the harbor at Troas. On the deck stood Paul and Silas, Timothy and Luke. They could still see the morning star in the sky as the boat lifted anchor and pulled away from the dock.

The slow summer wind had turned and now blew from the south. The current was good for a sail northwest. Soon the four men could see the distant mountains on the island of Samothracia, and there the ship dropped anchor for the night. The next morning, it sailed for Neapolis, the seaport of Philippi, in Macedonia.

Luke had been over the route before, and he told his companions a bit about the city to which they were headed.

"Long ago, silver and gold were mined in the mountains near Philippi," he said. "At that time, the city had another name. But it was renamed by Philip, the father of Alexander the Great. Later, the great battle between Augustus and Antony on one side and Brutus and Cassius on the other was fought nearby. The city was made a colony, and, in government, is really a 'little Rome,' but everyone calls it Philippi."

"What kind of people live there?" Paul wanted to know.

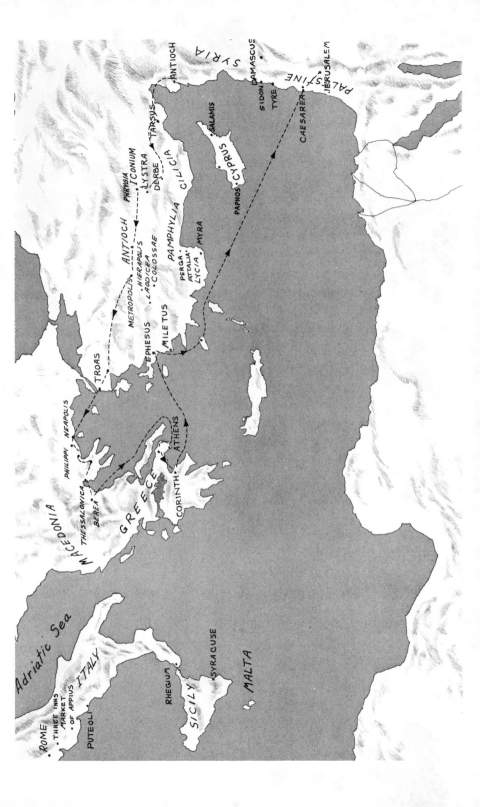

"Let me think." Luke was silent for a moment.

"There are really three kinds," he decided at last. "There are colonists from Rome who dominate the city. Then there are native Macedonians who make up the largest portion of the population. And there are Orientals from various sections of the East."

He looked at Paul.

"There are few Jews," he said.

Paul smiled.

"My orders are to preach to the Gentiles," he reminded Luke.

"Why then do you always preach to the Jews first?" Silas asked.

"The Jews at least know of the one true God," Paul answered.

He paused before he added, "And I still long to reach my own Jewish people and convince them that their only hope lies in faith in the Lord Jesus Christ."

Timothy had not been listening closely, but he had been using his eyes.

"Look!" he interrupted. "I can see land in the distance."

The four men turned to look, and Luke explained that they were seeing the mountains back of the port at Neapolis.

"Philippi is ten miles away, over those mountains," he said.

Soon the ship docked, and the four missionaries stood on land, the first followers of Jesus Christ ever to touch the soil of what is now called the continent of Europe.

They lost no time in locating the road to Philippi, but it was too late in the day to begin the journey inland.

The sea breeze made the night's rest pleasant, and the next morning the missionaries set out for Philippi. As they climbed the mountain, they could look back toward the sea and the coast where they had dropped anchor on their voyage. But each man was more interested in what lay beyond the mountains.

"Tell us more about Philippi," Timothy urged.

Luke told of the fortifications and buildings which the Romans had erected. He spoke, too, of temples to heathen gods and of a great Roman road which started at Neapolis and led westward five hundred miles inland.

As the four men passed the crest of the mountain and started down the other side, they saw a plain that seemed as level as the calm waters of the sea they had left behind.

"How green it is!" Silas exclaimed. "I can count several streams of water."

Luke smiled.

"Yes," he said. "Hundreds of years ago, this area was called 'The Place of Springs.' "

At last the city came into view, and the travelers sought rest for the night.

The next morning they made their plans.

"It is the sabbath day." Paul was thinking aloud.

"I have just remembered something," Luke said. "The few Jews who live here have a place for prayer outside the city on the bank of the Gangites River."

Soon Paul, Silas, Timothy, and Luke were walking through the city gate. When they found the place where the Jews met, Paul was amazed to see only a group of women.

"Women hold a more honored place here than in the East," Luke whispered to him.

The four missionaries joined in the service of praise to God and were invited to speak just as they would have been in a synagogue.

As he spoke of the Lord Jesus Christ, the long-promised Messiah of the Jews, Paul especially noticed one woman listening to him intently.

When the service was over, the woman introduced herself. "I am Lydia," she said, "a native of Thyatira, but I do not believe in the heathen gods worshiped there. I worship the one true God as do the Jews. I am a businesswoman. Will you come to my home and tell me and the women who work with me more about this Jesus, whom you say God raised from the dead?"

Paul and his companions accepted the invitation.

"In what business are you engaged?" Paul asked his hostess.

"I am a merchant," Lydia explained. "I sell the famous purple fabrics which skilled workers in my hometown know how to dye. The fabric is in great demand because it is used for the official toga at Rome and in the colonies."

Paul taught the women more and more about Jesus, and Lydia and her household became believers. They were baptized.

"If you are convinced that I am a real believer in the Lord Jesus, come and stay at my house," Lydia begged.

And for the rest of their time in Philippi, Paul and his companions made Lydia's house their home.

They continued to meet with the group which gathered to pray at the riverside. There they found many Gentiles who, like Lydia, believed in the one true God and did not accept heathen superstitions.

On their way to the place of prayer one day, the missionaries saw a pitiful girl following them.

"These men are servants of the most high God," she shouted. "They are telling you the way of salvation."

The people of Philippi were familiar with that Greek word translated "salvation." Sometimes they saw it carved on stones heaped by the roadside.

They knew that each such stone stood for a prayer to the gods for something a man desired deep in his heart. He wanted to feel safe and content.

The girl's voice was shrill, and as Paul turned and looked at her, he was sure that she was in the power of evil.

He asked Lydia about her.

"The poor woman is a slave," Lydia explained. "She belongs to a syndicate of men who make money out of her fortunetelling."

The next day the girl shouted the same words as Paul and Silas walked by. Another day the same thing happened.

At first Paul felt that the words of such a person were an insult to his gospel, but then he thought of something else.

"Jesus was interested in all kinds of people," he remembered. "He did not hesitate to help a sinful woman and a man who raved just as this girl is doing."

"The girl is possessed by an evil spirit," he told Lydia.

The next time he heard the familiar cry, Paul stopped in pity for the girl. He faced her and spoke to the evil spirit within her.

"I order you in the name of Jesus Christ to come out of her," he commanded.

Startled, the girl looked at him. Then, suddenly, she was quiet. The spirit of evil had left her.

When her owners saw that they could no longer make money out of their slave, they turned on Paul and Silas. They dragged them before the magistrate and charged them with disturbing the city.

"These men are Jews," they accused. "They teach customs which are not lawful for us Romans to practice."

News had come of troublesome Jews in the city of Rome, and a crowd joined in the attack.

Without investigating the charges, the magistrate ordered the two men stripped and beaten with rods. Blow after blow fell upon them.

They might have been beaten to death, but the magistrate, remembering Roman law, ordered Paul and Silas taken to prison and kept in safety.

The jailer took no chances. He threw them into the inner prison and fastened their feet in stocks.

At midnight, the other prisoners in that jail heard sounds they had never heard before.

Paul and Silas were praying and singing praises to God! One of the songs began:

> God is our refuge and strength,
> A very present help in trouble.[20]

Suddenly the prisoners felt the foundations of the prison quiver; then the ground shook. There was a great earthquake.

The doors of the prison flew open, and the stocks on the prisoners' feet fell apart.

The jailer awakened and came running.

When he saw that the prison doors were open, he drew his sword to kill himself. He well knew that Rome had penalties worse than death for a keeper who let prisoners escape.

Through the darkness of the dungeon, Paul saw the jailer in the moonlight and understood what he was about to do.

"Do not harm yourself," he shouted. "All your prisoners are here."

The jailer called for a light. Trembling with fear, he rushed into the inner prison and fell to his knees before Paul and Silas.

Paul put out his hand, and the jailer rose. Then he led the two missionaries out.

As he did so, he asked a question.

"What must I do to be saved?"

"You must believe in the Lord Jesus Christ," Paul answered. For he knew that the Lord Jesus could meet the deepest need of any man.

The jailer could hardly wait to hear more. He took the two men to his home and washed their wounds. Then Paul and Silas told him and his household about the Lord Jesus whom God had raised from the dead.

The jailer and his family became believers in Jesus. They were baptized.

They gave food to the two men, and Paul and Silas rejoiced with them in their new faith.

The next morning a guard brought orders from the magistrate that the two men were to be released.

Paul was indignant.

"We are Roman citizens," he protested. "These magistrates have beaten us publicly without a trial. Now they want to get rid of us secretly. Let them come themselves and take us out of the city."

The police stared in astonishment. Then they went running to the magistrate to report what Paul had said.

"Roman citizens!" the magistrate exclaimed. "Who would have believed that those two unimportant looking Jews had Roman citizenship?" He came at once and apologized to the two missionaries. Then he asked them to leave the city.

Paul and Silas agreed.

Before they left, they were careful to instruct the new Christians, and Timothy and Luke stayed on in Philippi to help the believers who often met together at Lydia's house.

20.
The Gospel Moves Westward

A famous road ran through the city of Philippi. It was the Egnatian Way, which the Romans had built years before.

Down this road Paul and Silas made their way.

They spent the first night at Amphipolis, often called "Nine Ways" because so many roads led into the city.

Paul and Silas kept to the Egnatian Way which wound between tall cliffs and the sea. Soon they could see a valley green with grass and olive orchards. Looking inland, they could see mountains covered with great forests.

The two men stopped in Amphipolis for only one night and then continued their journey, for they had decided to go to Thessalonica.

"It is a large city," Paul told Silas. "We can preach to many people, and the gospel of our Lord will spread to other places just as it has spread from the city of Jerusalem."

"Do you think Thessalonica will be like Jerusalem?" Silas asked.

"Of course not," Paul smiled.

"Thessalonica is largely Grecian in its ways. I hear that the Romans have classified it a free city and permit it to govern itself to a large extent. They even allow the magistrates of Thessalonica to inflict the death penalty without consulting them. There is no Roman garrison in the city, but it is a strong naval base. Of course the magistrates seek to enforce Roman laws, for they are eager to stand well with the government at Rome."

"What about the people and their religion?" Silas inquired.

"I am told that there are many Jews in the city," Paul answered. "Yet most of the people are heathen and worship the old gods you have heard about in Greek myths."

Paul and Silas were nearer the sea now. Soon they saw a city that seemed to rise from the waters of the gulf. It was Thessalonica.

The two missionaries entered the city gate and found lodging with a Jew named Jason.

The next day, Paul, as he usually did, went to a synagogue. He found it crowded, not only with Jews but with Grecian men and women who had turned from the superstitions of the Greeks and were seeking to worship the one true God.

For three weeks Paul preached to the people. He told them about Jesus whom God had raised from the dead, and he used the Jewish Scriptures to prove that this man from Nazareth was indeed the Messiah whom God had promised.

"This Jesus whom I preach unto you is the Christ," he declared plainly.

Paul preached not only in the synagogue. Daily he met with interested Greeks and Jews whenever they could find a quiet spot. He taught them, helping them to understand what it meant to be a follower of the Lord Jesus Christ.

Over and over again the Greeks asked a question which people all over the world wondered about, "What happens when a person dies?"

Paul had seen heathen funerals. He knew how sad and hopeless a heathen must have felt when someone he loved died.

"Christians do not grieve in the same way as people who have no hope," Paul told his listeners in Thessalonica. "We believe that Jesus died and that he rose from the dead.

"Believers in the Lord Jesus think of death as something like a sleep from which God will awaken them. Comfort each other with this faith."

The Christians in Thessalonica were learning to love each other and to live more happily. Especially were the women happier, for Paul taught that wives were not just to use for pleasure but to be loved and honored.

At night when the streets were quiet and there were no people with questions to be answered, passersby heard a dull thud, thud from the house of Jason.

Paul was weaving. He needed no light to work at his old trade. In the darkness, his sensitive fingers found the shuttle and counted the threads on the loom. In the shops by the sea, he could sell his finished tents and use the money to support himself.

Late one day a knock came on the door. Paul opened it and saw familiar faces.

"Timothy!" he exclaimed first. Then he welcomed other Christian friends who had come with Timothy from Philippi.

"The church at Philippi wants to help in the preaching of the gospel," the visitors told Paul. "We hear that you are working too hard. Use this for whatever you need, and give more of your time to preaching. Try to rest a bit."

They gave Paul a bag of money which the Christians in Philippi had sent to him. Paul thanked them, and the friends talked for a long time.

Paul asked about Lydia and other believers in Philippi, and he was glad for good news of their faith.

At last the visitors returned to their homes, but Timothy stayed in Thessalonica.

Because of the gift from the Christians in Philippi, Paul now had more time for preaching and teaching. He taught the Christian Way of living and urged believers to remember that Jesus was the supreme ruler of their lives. For by faith in him, they had become citizens of the kingdom of God.

When the strict Jews in Thessalonica saw prominent people accepting the Christian faith, they began to resent Paul and his work. As more and more people became believers, these Jews decided to get rid of the missionaries. They had heard Paul speak of "the kingdom of God," and the word "kingdom" suggested an easy way to twist what he had said. They began to whisper about the preacher.

"He is not loyal to Rome," they declared. "He could get all of us into trouble with the government."

Rumors about Paul grew and spread. One day a mob formed. More and more loafers joined it, and soon the crowd was storming the house of Jason, looking for Paul.

The missionaries were not there.

Angered yet more at their failure, the searchers seized Jason and dragged him before the city magistrates, charging him with harboring men who were disloyal to the Roman government.

"The men who are staying at Jason's house have turned the world upside down!" they shouted. "They are upsetting our city, and Jason has made them welcome. He has become a believer in one they call Christ, and along with them, he too says that there is another king, one named Jesus."

The charge of disturbing the peace and plotting against the government worried the magistrates, but they tried to be fair. They demanded that Jason and his friends make bond that there would be no trouble. Then they released the prisoners.

When Paul learned of the mob, he was distressed. He must not get his host into trouble, he decided. He talked the matter over with his fellow Christians.

That night he and his companions left for Berea.

In the synagogue there, they found a more open-minded group of Jews who listened eagerly to Paul's message. They were good Bible students and daily searched their Scripture scrolls to test the truth of what the preacher said.

Not only Jews but prominent Greeks listened, and many men and women believed in the Lord Jesus Christ.

News of the successful work Paul was doing traveled back to Thessalonica, and hostile Jews there decided to stop the preaching of the gospel in Berea. One day they came to the city.

"These preachers are the same men who stirred up Thessalonica," they told the Bereans. "Paul and his friends are not loyal citizens of Rome."

The believers paid no attention to the charges, but loafers and prejudiced people did, and the Christians, fearing for Paul's life, begged him to leave their city.

It was decided that Timothy and Silas should stay in Berea for a time to help the new believers.

One day some of the Berean Christians went with Paul down to the sea. There he saw a ship ready to sail for the port of Philippi where he had many friends. But Paul had no idea of turning back. Instead, he found a boat headed south for a city where men and women had never heard the gospel. He and his companions boarded a ship sailing for Athens, in southern Achaia.

21.
How Must I Begin?

As the ship left the coast of Macedonia, Paul and his companions stood on deck. Looking back, they saw the white clouds which hid the highest peak of Mount Olympus.

"That is supposed to be the home of the gods," someone remarked.

"Do educated Greeks still believe in the old superstitions?" Paul asked.

"Some of them do," the man answered, "especially in Athens. Yet many of them have cast aside their faith in the old gods and believe in nothing but their own wisdom."

"How can I reach these people with the gospel?" Paul wondered as the ship sailed on.

Most of the mountains of Macedonia could no longer be seen now, and soon even Olympus faded from sight. The ship had reached the Aegean, called "the sea of islands."

Paul and his friends talked of their work, and of how the gospel was spreading in Berea.

"Where did you go before you came to our town?" one of his companions asked.

Paul was glad to talk about some of his experiences. He told of seeing Jesus on the road to Damascus and of the church at Antioch in Syria, which had first set him apart to preach especially to the Gentiles. He mentioned the first missionary journey, and then he went on to tell about Derbe and Philippi and some of the other places he and Silas had visited on this second trip.

"Now there are churches of believers in the Lord Jesus in many cities," he said. "There is even a church in Lystra where I was once stoned."

His listeners encouraged him to talk about Philippi, for Paul seemed happiest when he spoke of his friends there.

"A woman named Lydia became a Christian in Philippi," Paul explained. "She was a great help to us. We stayed at her house. She did not stop with becoming a believer herself, but she was always doing something to help other people know about her Lord."

Paul smiled as he thought about Philippi.

"The church in Philippi even sent some of its members to visit me when I was in Thessalonica," he went on. "They brought me a gift. How I do thank God for my friends in Philippi."

The ship moved slowly, for the wind was gentle. There was much time for Paul and his companions to talk about the city to which they were sailing.

"Athens is a strange city, full of amazing statues," one man remarked.

"What is the religion there?" Paul inquired.

The man shook his head.

"Many of the people act as if they never heard of what we call religion," he replied. "You will find a strange mixture of teachings from mythology and from the old philosophers. Few people believe in the ancient gods, yet they have beautiful statues of them and often they worship before them." He paused for a moment and then continued.

"Most of these Greek people follow the teachings of either the Stoics or the Epicureans. The Stoics say that the world created itself and that nature is god. They condemn the worship of images, and they have some standards of self-discipline."

A Berean friend nodded. "Yes," he agreed, "I have heard about them. What about the Epicureans?"

Paul thought for a moment.

"Gamaliel, my old teacher, once spoke of that group," he said. "The Epicureans believe that the universe is an accident. They say the soul dies just as the body does and that the object of this life is to have what they call 'a good time.'

"Some of these Epicureans indulge all their physical appetites. Others live a little better morally, but their way of life is intensely selfish."

"Will these people be interested in the gospel of Jesus Christ?" the friend asked.

Paul sighed. "Neither group sounds as if it would be interested in a God of love and justice and mercy," he admitted. Yet he knew that he must preach to them.

As the ship approached Athens late one day, Paul stared in amazement at the beauty of the city. In the dim light, he could still see the tall marble columns of the Parthenon which stood on the Acropolis. Darkness had not yet closed in on the statue of Minerva.

"That is the old goddess of Athens," one of the Bereans explained. "She is called 'Athena' by the Greeks."

The ship docked, and Paul and his companions found a place to stay.

The next morning Paul went back to the dock with his friends, who would board a ship to go home. As they walked together, he reminded them again of a message he had given them to deliver.

"Tell Silas and Timothy to come to me as soon as they can."

The Bereans found a ship bound for Macedonia. They boarded it, and Paul watched it sail away. He stood on the dock until he could no longer see his friends waving at him.

Then, alone, he turned and made his way back toward the city.

As he did so, he looked about him with interest. In the darkness of the night before, he had not seen the great statue of the god Neptune which stood outside the gate.

Inside the city, he stopped in amazement to gaze at gleaming marble statues of the goddess Minerva and of the gods Jupiter, Apollo, and Mercury. Everywhere he looked, he saw skillfully carved statues.

Paul saw many temples too. One was dedicated to Bacchus, the god of wine and revelry.

The missionary shuddered at such idolatry. He thought of the great teachers of other centuries, men like Aristotle and Plato. As he looked at the city about him, he knew that the people of Athens in the first century after Christ were far, far different from those who had lived by the wisdom of Socrates and other thoughtful philosophers.

Paul made his way down the long street with covered markets. There were altars on every side and sanctuaries in every public building.

Often he stopped to read the Greek inscriptions. On one altar he read, "To the Unknown God."

Paul saw Romans and Greeks, Syrians and Egyptians. He saw merchants riding on donkeys with slaves running by their sides. He saw fathers leading their children past little shops where figs and dates and olives and goat cheese were sold. He saw bakers selling rich pastries and weavers fingering brightly colored embroideries.

No one spoke to him. He was alone in the great city of Athens.

Again he asked himself a question, "How can I make the people listen to the good news I have for them?"

Heartsick at the evidence of heathen worship on every hand, Paul was glad when someone told him of a synagogue in Athens.

On the sabbath day he went there and, as was his custom, he accepted the invitation to speak to the people. As he spoke of the Lord Jesus, he was glad to see among the Jewish worshipers a few Greeks who had turned from superstition to faith in the one true God.

The next day Paul went to the marketplace. He saw the Painted Porch of the Stoics. He saw little groups of people talking together. Paul joined a group, and when the opportunity came, he began to talk to them. The people listened to him, for all of them were curious about new ideas.

Paul told these heathen people about God who loved them and about Jesus who showed God's goodness and mercy. He told of Jesus' death and of his resurrection.

The people listened half-heartedly. "This man seems to be talking about a new god," some of them remarked.

"A new god?" others questioned. They pricked up their ears. "Let's hear what he is saying."

They took Paul's arm and led him to the Areopagus. "This is where our judges meet," they said, pointing to the seats hewn out of stone. "You speak of new things. Tell us more about your religion and that strange god you talk about."

Paul looked at the crowd. He saw both native Athenians and foreigners who lived in the city. How could he make them understand?

With a prayer in his heart, he walked to the center of the amphitheater. There, in a famous Grecian city, near a hill named for Mars, the Roman god of war, he must preach the gospel of peace through Jesus Christ. How would he begin?

22.
The God Who Is Different

As Paul stood in the great amphitheater at Athens, he faced a crowd who knew nothing of the one true God about whom he had learned as a child. These people had never even heard the name of the Lord Jesus Christ whom he trusted and sought to serve each day. How could he begin to make them understand what it meant to worship the Lord God?

Paul thought of the many altars and temples and statues of gods which he had seen on the streets. Suddenly he realized that these people were not satisfied with their religion. They were seeking for something. He knew how he would begin his sermon.

"Men of Athens," he said, "I can see from your city that you are very religious.

"And as I looked at your statues and altars and sanctuaries and saw you at worship, I found one altar with this inscription:

To the Unkown God

"Let me tell you about this God whom you do not know. He is the true God, and he is different from any god men have ever thought up."

The people leaned forward to hear better, and Paul continued to speak.

"This true God, who made the world and all that is in it, is Lord of heaven and earth. He does not live in

153

temples which men build with their hands.

"Neither is he represented by objects fashioned by men's fingers, no matter how much skill they have.

"He is the one true God whom you do not know, and he gives to all life and breath and all things.

"Of one blood, this God who is different has made all nations of men who dwell on the earth. He has decided when and where they shall be born.

"He has put into their hearts the desire to know him so that they may seek him and find him and know that he is not far from any one of us.

"In this God we live, and move, and have our being, as certain of your own poets have said: 'For we are his children. He created us.' "

The Greeks smiled as they recognized the old poem, and Paul continued.

"Because we are made in the image of God, we ought never to think that he is like a statue of gold or silver or stone, carved by men's fingers.

"God has been patient with people for many years, but now he calls on men everywhere to turn to him and change their ways.

"He has sent the Lord Jesus into the world to redeem it, and this same Lord Jesus will someday judge each one of us.

"God has guaranteed this by raising Jesus from the dead."

At the mention of a man raised from the dead, Paul heard laughter break out in the crowd. Some of his listeners were making fun of his message.

"We will hear you again about this matter," others said.

It was no use to keep on speaking, for the crowd was buzzing.

Slowly, Paul turned and started down the hill.

A few men followed him asking questions. Paul taught them and others from day to day. Some of them believed in the Lord Jesus. Among these believers were Dionysius, one of the members of the Areopagus, and a woman named Damaris.

Paul thought about the situation in Athens.

"These are the most cultured people in the world," he decided. "They are among the best educated. Yet they have never even dreamed of a god like the righteous and loving One who reveals himself in Jesus Christ.

"Most of these Athenians think of the gods they worship as not being as moral and honest as some of their old philosophers."

In his mind Paul could see the marble statues and stately temples of the city. He admired their loveliness of form and design, but he shuddered at the twisted ideas of God which they represented.

Paul shook his head.

Would the people of Athens ever learn the beauty of holiness?

"Most of these people are intelligent," he thought. "Yet they are all alike in their ignorance of the one true God and of how a man can worship him."

Paul's heart ached for these people. He was discouraged and seemed to be accomplishing nothing in Athens. He longed to talk with Timothy and Silas who had not yet come to him.

At last his mind turned to other parts of Greece which had never heard the gospel. He began to ask questions about other cities.

One day Dionysius told him about Corinth.

"It is the capital of the Roman province of Achaia,"

he said, "but it is not a free city like Athens. Corinth was practically destroyed when the Romans conquered the world, but less than a hundred years ago, Julius Caesar sent a colony of Romans to rebuild it. It has a strategic location on the isthmus between the Aegean and Adriatic Seas, and it is important from both a military and commercial point of view.

"When the city was rebuilt, many of the Greek merchants returned. It is now a wealthy center where business flourishes. Its location on the isthmus connecting northern and southern Greece makes it a natural place for trade and commerce."

"Do you think the people of Corinth would be more likely to receive the gospel than the people of Athens have been?" Paul asked.

"I do not know," Dionysius replied, "but at least they would be different. Neither the Greeks nor the Romans in Corinth think as much about the old gods or the philosophers as do the people here in Athens."

"What are their interests?" Paul wanted to know.

"They are largely interested in making money and enjoying themselves," Dionysius answered.

Paul prayed to know what he should do next. He thought of the crowds on the busy streets of Corinth. He would find Jews there, he knew, and maybe a synagogue. Yet perhaps not even one man in Corinth had ever heard of the Lord Jesus Christ.

Paul made his decision.

"I will go to Corinth," he told Dionysius one day. "How do I get there?"

"You can easily find a ship sailing for the harbor of Cenchrea on the eastern side of the isthmus," Dionysius said. "Corinth is only seven miles from that port."

Paul made his plans.

"Be on the lookout for my friends, Luke and Timothy, when they come," he told Dionysius. "They will expect to find me in the synagogue of the Jews, and you can tell them to come on to Corinth."

Soon Paul told Dionysius and Damaris and the other believers good-by. He went down to the sea and found a ship bound for Cenchrea.

Alone, he sailed away from Athens.

As he looked back at the city, he saw the Parthenon standing high on the Acropolis, and he remembered the many, many altars and sanctuaries to the old gods of the myths.

Paul thought of the people with their fine minds and cultural opportunities, and he sighed.

For he knew that he was leaving in Athens only a few people who worshiped the true God and even fewer who were believers in the Lord Jesus Christ.

23.
On the Bridge of the Sea

As the ship bound for Cenchrea sailed south, Paul watched a gull flying high above the calm, blue waters. His soul was strangely comforted. When night came, he looked up at the stars and remembered that the God whose glory filled the heavens is the same God who is always near.

Along with his usual nighttime worship, Paul whispered a prayer for forgiveness for his anxiety and fretfulness in Athens. Here, where there were no reminders of heathen gods and idolatry, he could better sense the steadying assurance of the glory of God in Christ Jesus.

With deep gratitude in his heart, Paul remembered the voice that had sent him to preach the gospel to the Gentiles. He thought too of the promise of Jesus which he had already found true, "Lo, I am with you always."

Paul slept well. The next morning, he awoke to the smell of salt air and the sight of a bit of greenness in the distance. As the ship neared Cenchrea, he saw rich foliage and high hills.

The harbor of Cenchrea was a busy place. Paul watched ships unloading freight to be carried overland to a port on the other side of the isthmus. There it would be picked up by other ships or carried inland by slow caravan. No good sailor wanted to risk the storms that threatened a ship that attempted to sail around the southern tip of Achaia.

Paul saw one small ship being dragged overland across the isthmus. "It will be launched again on the other side," someone told him.

"They say that the emperor plans to have a ship canal dug across the isthmus," a traveler from Rome remarked.

The sailors laughed. "Such a project is unthinkable!" they said.

As Paul walked up the road toward Corinth, he saw in the distance a great mountain of rock towering two thousand feet above the sea. It was the Acrocorinthus, and Paul knew that the city lay at its base. Soon he reached Corinth.

As he made his way through the streets, Paul saw shops with marble guttering and mosaic floors. There were booths for workers with gold and silver and for makers of porcelain. There were shops for selling cloth and for dyeing it. In one of these Paul saw workers using the famous dyes made from mollusk shells from Tyre. The color reminded him of the royal purple cloth which Lydia sold in Philippi.

Entering one shop, Paul noticed a loom. He saw a Jewish weaver.

Paul introduced himself and told the man he was a native of Tarsus, in Cilicia.

"That is where we get the finest goat hair for our tents," the weaver said.

Then he told Paul his name, "I am Aquila. My wife and I have this shop."

He pointed to a woman at another loom. "This is my wife, Priscilla. We are natives of Pontus but came here sometime ago from Rome."

Paul did not need to ask why Priscilla and Aquila

had left Rome. He knew that Emperor Claudius had banished all Jews from the Imperial City.

"Do you find business good here?" Paul asked.

"Indeed we do," Aquila replied. "We cannot make enough tents to keep up with the demand, especially when people come to watch the games on the isthmus."

Paul smiled.

"I, too, am a weaver," he said. "As a boy I learned to make tents and have done so many times since I grew up. I have not forgotten my trade."

He waited a moment and then asked, "May I work with you?"

"Indeed you may," Aquila replied. "Priscilla and I have living quarters back of our shop, and you may stay there with us."

Paul set to work the next morning. Though his fingers had lost none of their skill, sometimes they ached from the unaccustomed activity. But Paul kept on weaving. He made good tents, and Aquila and Priscilla were delighted with his work.

One day the three friends climbed the steep path that led to the top of Acrocorinthus, the great stony mountain that rose above the city.

"It has never been necessary to have a garrison to defend this place," Aquila explained. "It is a natural fortress, reached only by narrow paths which a few soldiers can guard."

As he stood on the highest peak of the mountain, Paul understood why the isthmus was called "the bridge of the sea."

"The land looks like a narrow bridge across the water," he said. "It connects northern and southern Greece just as a bridge might do."

It was a clear day, and as Paul and his companions looked east, they could see the Acropolis at Athens. On both sides of them was water, with ships sailing east and west. Below them was the narrow plain between the seas.

"Look!" Priscilla exclaimed. "We can even see a heavily loaded caravan of camels."

"No wonder Corinth is a busy place," Paul said. "It is the spot where the sea lanes meet the road across the land."

Another day, Paul's friends asked him whether he would like to see the bema.

"The bema?" he questioned.

They led him to a courtroom near the center of the marketplace. Paul noted the richly ornamented walls and the benches where both witnesses and prisoners sat, waiting to give testimony and to receive sentence.

On the street again, Aquila pointed out the old temple to Apollo, with its Greek columns, and the many places of amusement throughout the city. Paul counted thirty-three night clubs.

On sabbath days, the three friends went to the synagogue. There, as he had done in other places, Paul found both Jews and Gentiles who worshiped the one true God. Once more he began to tell the people about the Lord Jesus.

Both in the synagogue and as they talked with Paul at home, Aquila and Priscilla learned what it meant to be a Christian. They became believers in Christ.

Just as Paul was helping them in their work, they began to help him with his.

"We are laborers together with God," Paul told them.

One day travelers came to the door of Aquila's shop

and inquired for Paul. Paul looked up from his loom. He rubbed his eyes for a moment. Then he bounded across the room.

"Silas! Timothy!" he shouted.

"These are my friends who have been working in Berea," he told Aquila and Priscilla.

There was no more weaving for Paul that day.

He asked about the work in Berea and in Thessalonica, and Silas and Timothy reported growing churches in both places.

"Those believers, especially in Thessalonica, think so much of you," they told Paul. "They need to be encouraged and strengthened to live as Christians."

"I have been wanting to write them," Paul said, "but I have been having trouble with my eyes. It is hard for me to form the letters."

Timothy smiled.

"I will be glad to do the writing for you," he offered. "You tell me what to say."

The next day Timothy brought brush and ink and some sheets of parchment. As Paul sat at his loom, he thought of Thessalonica and told Timothy what to put in the letter.

"We'll all use our Roman names," he said. Timothy and Silas agreed, and Timothy wrote each word carefully. The letter began:

> From Paul, Silvanus, and Timothy—
> To the people of the church in Thessalonica, who belong to God the Father and the Lord Jesus Christ:

> May grace and peace be yours. We always thank God for you all, and mention you in our prayers.[21]

Each day Timothy got out his writing materials and wrote the message which Paul dictated to him. Paul did not forget to mention the good example the Thessalonians had set for the other Christians in Macedonia in helping to spread the gospel. He tried to say something that would help them to be good followers of the Lord Jesus. He said:

> Remember, God has taught you to love one another.
> Study to be quiet.
> Attend strictly to your own affairs.
> Keep busy at your work.
> Live in honesty and in purity.
> Rejoice in the Lord.
> In everything give thanks;
> for this is the will of God in Christ Jesus for you.
> The grace of our Lord Jesus Christ be with you.

This letter Paul wrote is in the Bible. In mine it is headed:

THE FIRST LETTER OF PAUL THE APOSTLE
TO THE
THESSALONIANS

24.
Ambassadors for Christ

In the ruins of ancient Corinth, archaeologists have found an old, old stone on which is carved the inscription:

SYNAGOGUE OF THE JEWS

Some students think this stone may have been a part of the synagogue where Paul was preaching in the year A.D. 50 or 51 when Gallio was the Roman governor of the province of Achaia with headquarters at Corinth.

To the Jews of that city, Paul said over and over again, "Jesus is the Christ." And to all of the people he said, "This Jesus whom God raised from the dead is the Savior."

So well did Paul witness to his Lord that many people in Corinth, both Jews and Greeks, became Christians. Even Crispus, the ruler of the synagogue, believed in the Lord Jesus Christ.

The strict Jews began to grumble.

"If Paul keeps on preaching, many other Jewish people may accept the Christian faith," they said. They began to argue violently with Paul. Arguments grew into more active opposition, and opposition into personal charges against him.

The trouble came to a head one day as Paul was

165

speaking in the synagogue. After his opponents had made some particularly vicious remarks about him and his work, Paul threw aside his outer coat and shook it fiercely at the men who were tormenting him.

His Jewish listeners knew what that gesture meant. For this was an old custom, by which a man said, "Just as I shake the dust from off this garment, so I am ridding myself of all association with you."

He put this meaning into words when he said, "Your blood be upon your own heads. I am innocent, for I have brought you God's call to faith in the Lord Jesus. From now on I will preach to the Gentiles." He walked out of the room.

For a moment, no one moved. Then Silas and Timothy, Aquila and Priscilla, and other believers, both Jews and Gentiles, followed the preacher. Even Crispus left his seat as ruler of the synagogue and followed Paul out of the building.

"Where can we go?" these Christians asked.

"You can meet at my house," Titus Justus offered. "It is next door to the synagogue."

So Paul and the other believers, both Jews and Gentiles, met in the home of a Roman in the Greek city of Corinth. There Paul continued to preach, and many other people in Corinth became believers.

Yet Paul was worried. The Jews in the synagogue were keeping strict watch on the Christians. They saw the crowds growing and heard that more and more people were declaring their faith in Jesus Christ. Paul remembered his experiences with Jewish troublemakers in other cities. He had been the victim of their plots. What would they do to him here in Corinth?

Anxiety grew into fear. Would he get hurt? Paul knew how it felt to be beaten with clubs and thrown into prison. He thought of work yet to be done for his

Lord. He wanted to preach the gospel in so many places. Aquila and Priscilla had told him of Rome where there were only a handful of Christians. Paul wanted to preach the gospel in the Imperial City and in many other places.

One night, when it was hard to relax and sleep, Paul had a vision. Again he heard the beloved voice that had spoken to him years before.

"You need not be afraid, Paul," the Lord Jesus assured him. "I am with you, and I have many followers in this city. No one shall hurt you here. Go on preaching the gospel."

By the next morning the anxiety was gone. Paul kept on preaching, and more and more people became Christians.

The Jews waited. One day they had Paul arrested and taken before Gallio, the Roman governor.

"This man is persuading people to worship God contrary to the law," they charged.

Paul was about to defend his position when Gallio spoke sharply.

"This is not a matter of Roman law," he said. "If a crime had been committed, I would give attention to it. I cannot waste time on religious disputes like this. The case is dismissed." And he ordered Paul's accusers to leave the courtroom.

Again Paul was free to preach, and this he did. For many days he instructed the Christians who met at the house of Titus Justus. And always his sermon included one great message: "The Lord Jesus was crucified, but God raised him from the dead. He is the Savior of all who believe in him, both Gentiles and Jews."

More and more people became Christians. The church in Corinth was growing.

Yet Paul was not satisfied with what he was doing.
He often thought of the Christians in new churches
in other cities, especially of those in Thessalonica.
They needed teaching. He wrote another letter to
them. In the Bible, this letter is called The Second
Letter of Paul the Apostle to the Thessalonians.

Paul was thinking, too, of Jerusalem, where there
were men and women who had known Jesus. He
thought of Antioch in Syria, the city which had first
given the name *Christian* to believers in the Lord
Jesus Christ. He thought of Barnabas and other
friends in the church there, friends who had prayed
for him and set him apart for the work of preaching
to the Gentiles. He needed their encouragement and
advice.

One day he talked matters over with Timothy and
Silas and some of the other Christians in Corinth.

"The church here seems to be doing well," he said.
"I think I should leave and go back to Antioch for a
time. I keep thinking about cities which have not yet
heard the gospel. I must plan to preach in other
places."

His friends did not argue with him. They understood his longing for people in many places to hear
the gospel.

"We will go part of the way with you," Aquila and
Priscilla offered.

It was springtime now, and the snows had melted
from the lowlands of the isthmus. One morning Paul
and Aquila and Priscilla made their way to the port at
Cenchrea. Looking back, they could still see the snow-
capped peak of the Acrocorinthus behind the city.

Boarding a ship, they sailed across the Aegean, east
to Ephesus, for Paul wanted to see what opportunities
that city offered for preaching the gospel. He went to

the synagogue and found the Jews quite interested in his message. They begged him to stay.

"I will return to you if God wills," Paul promised. "And Aquila and Priscilla will remain here for a time."

One morning he found a ship sailing for Caesarea, a port in Palestine. From there a road led south to Jerusalem.

Paul boarded that ship and set sail.

There was time to recall all that had taken place on this second missionary journey. Paul thought of his seeming failure in Athens, and he sighed. Then he remembered the new churches in Philippi and Thessalonica, in Berea and in Corinth. He smiled as he thought of Lydia and Titus Justus and other friends in these places. Paul thanked God for every one of them. He thanked God for the new churches where the gospel of Jesus Christ was being preached and where men and women were learning to live each day as Jesus had taught. In spite of their mistakes, these new Christians were telling others about their Lord. Paul thought of them, along with Timothy and Silas and his preacher friends, and he said softly to himself, "We are ambassadors for Christ."

Paul remembered the weaknesses and mistakes of these Christians. He thought of his own weaknesses. His message was sometimes blunt, and his heart was sometimes afraid. Yet great joy filled his soul because God had used him to proclaim the glad, glad news of salvation.

Gratefully Paul remembered the night his Lord had spoken to him in Corinth when he was full of fear, and he whispered a prayer:

Thanks be unto God for his unspeakable gift.[22]

25.
A Famous Letter

"What must I do next? In what new city must I preach?"

Over and over these questions had pounded in Paul's thoughts. They were still there as the ship docked at Caesarea. They traveled with him as he made a short visit in Jerusalem and then went up to Antioch, in Syria. Should he go to Ephesus now? One day he asked some of his friends in Antioch about it.

"Ephesus is one of the three great cities of the eastern Mediterranean," they reminded him. "There you will find both Greeks and Romans living by their heathen customs, worshiping heathen gods."

Paul nodded his head. "I know," he said. "I saw their great temple to the goddess Diana, but there are some Jews in Ephesus too. I spoke in their synagogue, and they begged me to stay and teach them more about our Lord. I promised to return if it be God's will."

He and his friends prayed that he might know and do that will, and at last Paul reached a decision.

"I will go to Ephesus," he announced, "but first I must help the believers in Galatia and Phrygia. I hear they are having trouble in the churches there."

The trip to help those churches did not mean a pleasant sail, as the trip to Ephesus would have been. Instead, it meant climbing the steep slopes of the

Taurus Mountains and walking the hot roads to Derbe and Lystra, to Iconium, and on to Antioch in Pisidia.

Paul set out on his journey. In every town he rejoiced in finding churches where the gospel of Jesus Christ was being preached. Yet he was troubled. It seemed so difficult for these people to know and to follow the Christian Way. They had many heathen habits and customs. They needed so much teaching. Everywhere Paul went, he helped to strengthen the faith of the believers.

After visiting Antioch in Pisidia, he continued on to Ephesus. He was an older man than when he first walked the Egnatian Road and the miles seemed longer, but at last he reached Ephesus.

It was good to see Aquila and Priscilla and Timothy and the other believers. Again Paul preached in the synagogue, but the Jews did not listen with the sympathy he had found on his first visit. So the Christians moved their meetings to the school of Tyrannus, and there Paul taught them every day. For three years, he made his headquarters at Ephesus.

Again he saw the great temple built to honor Diana, and it reminded him of heathen temples in Galatia and in Greece. He knew the believers in those countries were facing the same problems as the Christians in Ephesus.

"They want to live as Christians should," he told Timothy one day, "but so often they are trapped in the evils of pagan habits. They have been reared to observe heathen customs. Even their ideas of God are often heathen."

Visitors came one day and told Paul of conditions in Corinth. "The believers are even quarreling among themselves," they reported. "Some say you were the best teacher they ever had; others side with Apollos."

Paul shook his head. "They seem to forget that both of us are only messengers of Christ," he said. "I did my best to preach his gospel in Corinth. I did not depend on my own ability but sought to teach people the wisdom of God. No man has anything to boast about. It is God who works in us, for we are his."

"It would help if you could talk with the believers in Corinth," the visitors assured Paul.

"I cannot go to Corinth just yet," he replied.

He told his friends in Ephesus about the situation in Corinth. "Will you help me to write a letter to the church there?" he asked one day.

Timothy agreed, and so did other friends.

Letter writing was a difficult task in the first century A.D. It was particularly difficult for Paul because his eyesight was not good and he was so busy preaching the gospel.

His friends prepared for the task. Perhaps Stephanas and Fortunatus collected animal skins from which the hair had been scraped and the surface rubbed smooth like paper. They cut these skins into sheets and fastened them together into a long scroll. Someone brought a reed pen. Perhaps two friends mixed the soot and liquid gum for the ink. At last everything was ready.

Paul dictated the words, and Timothy wrote them on the parchment, forming each Greek letter with care.

Paul had prayed about the Corinthians and their problems. He tried to think of each question in a practical way and make some suggestions for its solution. Yet he realized he could never make rules about all that a man did. He could never anticipate all the problems a Christian must face.

"The Lord Jesus did not give many rules," he said to himself. "I must tell these people something that will help them to live as Christians no matter what comes to them."

He may have realized that Christians in other places might read his letter, for he addressed it not only to the church at Corinth, but to "all that in every place call upon the name of Jesus Christ our Lord."

Paul could never have dreamed that this letter would help Christians around a world so much larger than anyone knew in his day. He had no idea that his letter would come down through the centuries as a part of the Bible and be translated into more than a thousand languages and dialects.

Yet he was careful to let the Holy Spirit guide his thinking as he wrote to the church at Corinth.

In that letter is one of the most famous passages in the whole Bible. In the thirteenth chapter of First Corinthians are Paul's words about the kind of love God can put into a believer's heart, a kind of love that can be trusted to make its own rules. It is the kind of love that can solve problems.

Love is patient and kind; love is not jealous, or conceited, or proud; love is not ill-mannered, or selfish, or irritable; love does not keep a record of wrongs; love is not happy with evil, but is happy with the truth. Love never gives up: its faith, hope, and patience never fail.

Love is eternal. . . . Meanwhile these three remain: faith, hope, and love; and the greatest of these is love.[23]

In his letter, Paul told his friends in Corinth of his plans to stay in Ephesus for a while. He promised to make them a visit later. He remembered to include greetings from Aquila and Priscilla and the church that met in their house.

When the letter was finished, Paul signed it with his own hand and added a benediction.

The grace of the Lord Jesus be with you. My love be with you all in Christ Jesus.[24]

Now he must find a traveler to carry the letter to Corinth.

26.
A Temple Paul Saw

Paul sighed with relief when his letter to the church at Corinth was completed. He thanked his friends for their help in writing it, and he was especially glad when one of them reported that he had found someone to carry the letter to Corinth.

Timothy rolled the scroll carefully and wrapped it in linen cloth. Then he turned to Paul.

"Perhaps you can rest some now," he said. "Let's go for a walk."

For a moment Paul was tempted to refuse. There were other letters to write, he knew. The churches in Galatia, especially, needed advice. And more and more new believers were joining the church in Ephesus. Paul rejoiced in every Christian, but he understood that each new believer meant another person who must be taught how to live the Christian Way. And that Way was very different from the heathen way.

"Let's go for a walk," Timothy repeated, for Paul had seemed not to hear his suggestion.

Paul smiled as he agreed, and together the two friends walked down the long street paved with marble and on to the temple of Diana.

It was a magnificent building, later listed as one of the seven wonders of the world. Timothy and Paul measured the tall columns with their eyes and rubbed their fingers over the smooth marble stones skillfully fitted together to make the walls. They knew that inside was a huge, ugly statue of the goddess Diana whom the Greeks called Artemis. The Ephesians said that the statue had fallen from the heavens.

"The Greeks worshiped Diana a long time ago, didn't they?" Paul asked.

"Yes," Timothy replied, "but their goddess was very different from this one. She was goddess of the hunt, and there was no immorality connected with her worship. This Diana is the patroness of Ephesus, and the people think of her as sponsoring all sorts of evil deeds in the name of religion."

Paul was studying the building thoughtfully. "It is said that it took one hundred twenty years to erect it," he told Timothy.

"It is operated by a large landholding company here in Ephesus," Timothy said, "but people all over Asia join in the worship of Diana. Hundreds of priests and thousands of women serve in this temple."

Paul did not reply, and Timothy turned to see whether he had heard his explanation. He saw that his friend was no longer looking at the temple. He seemed to be gazing back into the city.

"What do you see, Paul?" Timothy asked.

Paul smiled. "In my mind, I see another temple in Ephesus," he said. "In this city, our Lord is building a church. It has no columns or walls that a man can see or touch. It has not even a house in which to meet, but the Lord Jesus himself is its foundation. Each believer is like a living stone which he will fit into place. And in these believers, his Spirit will live and rule as in a temple."

Timothy did not quite understand. His mind was still busy with the temple of Diana.

"Have you seen the little shrines which the silversmiths make and sell?" he asked Paul. "They look almost like the big statue inside the temple. The silversmiths make a great deal of money from their sales."

Paul shook his head. "I have not even heard about them," he replied.

The two men went home, and soon Timothy and Erastus left to help the churches in Macedonia.

Paul went back to his preaching, and people continued to accept the faith of the Lord Jesus. Some who had fooled the people with deceitful tricks gave up this way of making money and burned their evil books which played on ignorance and superstition. And the cause of Christ grew in this heathen city.

Yet Paul was not content. The care of the new Christians in all the churches was heavy on his heart, and he wrote a letter to the churches in Galatia, reminding them that a believer must not only trust in the grace of God, he must live by the faith which he professes.

In that letter, Paul tried to share his own experience with Christians in Galatia. He said:

Christ liveth in me:
and the life which I now live . . .
I live by faith of the Son of God,
who loved me, and gave himself for me.[25]

These words are near the end of the second chapter of the Epistle to the Galatians for this letter, too, became a part of the Bible.

Paul may have been writing when someone told him that two of his friends had been arrested and taken before a Roman officer.

Paul rose from his chair. "What happened?" he asked.

"It seems that a silversmith named Demetrius called a meeting of his union," the messenger said. "He reminded the men that the sale of shrines to Diana had been getting smaller and smaller.

" 'This is the way we make our money,' Demetrius told the silversmiths. 'This man Paul has persuaded many people that these are not real gods which we make. Our business is in danger and so is the temple of Diana.' Immediately a mob formed."

The messenger paused a moment for breath. Then he continued.

"I think the mob was looking for you, Paul. Instead, they found Gaius and Aristarchus and dragged them away."

Paul was already on his way to the town hall. As he drew nearer, he heard the shouts of the mob, "Great is Diana of the Ephesians!" The whole city seemed full of confusion.

As Paul was about to enter the room, a friend held him back. "Wait a moment," he said.

The two men saw the mob push forward a Jew named Alexander. Did they mistake him for Paul?

Alexander started to explain, but the shouts of the mob drowned his voice.

Again Paul heard the clamor, "Great is Diana of the Ephesians!"

The Roman clerk had been talking to Demetrius. He held up his hand to quiet the shouting.

"Calm down," he ordered. "Everyone knows that the people of Ephesus worship the goddess Diana. These men have not robbed your temple or insulted the goddess."

He turned to Demetrius. "If you or your craftsmen have any just complaint, get a lawyer, and let the matter be argued in court."

He looked at the mob sternly. "You know that Rome does not countenance uproars like this," he said. "Ephesus may have to account for such a gathering."

Demetrius and the mob slunk away.

Paul breathed a sigh of relief. The town clerk had not allowed his sense of justice to be swayed by those silversmiths, even though they represented money-making trades. Perhaps Roman law would protect the Christians in Ephesus from the unjust attacks of their enemies.

"I must hasten to finish my work here," Paul told the believers one day. "I feel that I must preach in Rome, but first I must go to several other places."

Soon he told the Christians in Ephesus good-by. Again he reminded them that they belonged to the Lord Jesus and that in their hearts the Holy Spirit of God lived as in a temple. If he ruled in their lives, the church would keep on growing.

Yet even Paul would have been amazed had he known how strong the influence of that church of Jesus Christ would become and how far into the future its influence would reach.

Three hundred years later the great temple of Diana lay in ruins, and even later, the entire city of Ephesus was gone. More than a thousand years later, archaeologists found in the ruins of an Ephesian gateway a rough stone on which had once rested a statue of Diana or Artemis. Cut into the stone was a crude cross and an inscription written in Greek.

DEMEAS HAS REMOVED THE DECEITFUL IMAGE OF THE DEMON ARTEMIS AND IN ITS PLACE PUT THIS SIGN WHICH DRIVES AWAY THE IDOLS, TO THE PRAISE OF GOD AND OF THE CROSS, THE VICTORIOUS, IMPERISHABLE SYMBOL OF CHRIST.*

---

* *The Interpreter's Dictionary of the Bible* (New York: Abingdon Press, 1962), II, p. 118. Used by permission.

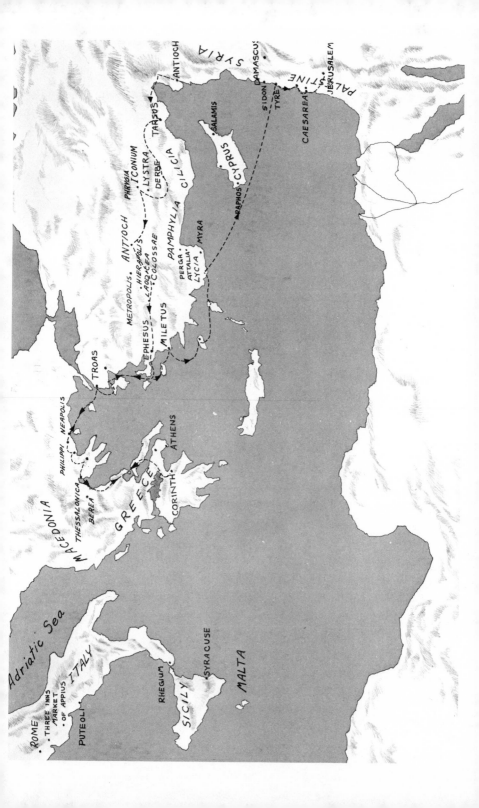

27.
A Homesick Traveler

Again Paul was planning to go on a trip. "I must preach in Rome," he told his friends as he left Ephesus, "but first I must go to Macedonia and to Corinth and to several other places to encourage the believers in the new churches in this part of the world. Then I would like to go to Jerusalem for the Passover."

The visit to places where he had preached and where churches had been formed was something of a good-by tour for Paul. Preaching in Rome would probably mean that he would not travel in these countries again. Yet he was alert to the needs of the believers not only here but in Judea. There the need for food was acute.

Wherever he went on this trip, Paul told the Gentile churches of the needy Christians in and about Jerusalem. He had never asked money for his own expenses, but he did not hesitate to ask it for these needy believers. He was glad to see that these Gentile church members joyfully shared what they had with Christians they had never seen.

It was wintertime when Paul reached Corinth, and he stayed there for three months. He was both saddened and indignant to find that some of the church members there had fallen into their old heathen habits of immoral living. He did all he could to help them, but his mind was filled with thoughts of preaching in Rome. He had heard how loyal the Christians there were to what they understood of the gospel, but he knew that they needed much teaching. Then, too, there were so many people in Rome who had never even heard the gospel.

For three months Paul stayed in Corinth, in the home of Gaius, preaching, counseling, and thinking. He decided to send a letter to the Christians in Rome. Tertius, a member of the Corinthian church, was a good scribe, and he would do the actual writing.

One day Paul began his letter, a letter which was to be preserved in the Bible as the Epistle to the Romans. It was to become one of Paul's most famous letters.

Some students think that this epistle was written as a circular letter and copies made with the name of a certain place put in each one and personal references adjusted. One copy went to the church at Rome.

In that letter to the Romans, Paul introduced himself as "a servant of Jesus Christ" called to preach the gospel to many nations.

He told these Romans how much he thanked God for their faith. "I always pray for you," he said. "I earnestly ask that God will let me come to you. For a long time I have wanted to do this because I am eager to preach the gospel in Rome."

Paul wrote:

"I am not ashamed of the gospel of Christ:
for it is the power of God unto salvation to
every one that believeth." [26]

Paul knew that believers in Rome were finding it difficult to live the Christian Way. He confessed that he himself often had trouble doing this. "Sometimes it seems that two men are fighting within me," he wrote. "One is delighted to do the will of God. The other wants to do selfish things."

Paul went on to tell those Christians at Rome about the grace and goodness of God and the wonder of his love. As he thought of perils he had faced, of the stonings and beatings and imprisonments and discouragements, he wrote:

> We know that in everything God works for good with those who love him.[27]

Paul remembered enemies who had tried to thwart his preaching of the gospel, who had threatened him and started false rumors about him, and he asked a question, "Who shall separate us from the love of Christ?"

Paul recalled frustrations and persecutions, illness and fatigue. He thought of famines and of threatening enemies, of danger and of death itself, and he wrote:

> In all these things we are more than conquerors through him that loved us.
> For I am persuaded, that neither death, nor life, nor angels, nor principalities, nor powers, nor things present, nor things to come, nor height, nor depth, nor any other creature, shall be able to separate us from the love of God, which is in Christ Jesus our Lord.[28]

All these things are mentioned in the last part of the eighth chapter of the Book of Romans in your Bible.

Paul may have been telling Tertius how to finish this letter when friends brought him news that his

old enemies in Corinth had learned of his plan to sail
to Syria and were plotting to kill him. Quickly he
and Luke left the city by another route and went
briefly to Philippi. Other friends, who had planned to
go with him to Jerusalem, sailed with Timothy to
Troas. There Paul met them five days later.

It was a joy to him to find a growing church of
the Lord Jesus in Troas. For a week, Paul and his
companions had fellowship with the believers there.
They talked and worshiped together and ate the
Lord's Supper which Jesus had asked his followers
to observe in his memory. Then Paul and his companions continued on their journey.

It was now too late to reach Jerusalem for the
Passover, but Paul wanted very much to be there for
the Feast of Pentecost. He was weary of heathen
scenes and celebrations, and he was homesick for
the familiar sights and customs of Jerusalem. The
Feast of Pentecost was a thanksgiving harvest festival of the Jewish people. The observances began
when the first sheaf of barley was cut and ended with
the harvesting of the wheat. Jewish farmers brought
their newly-cut sheaves and waved them before the
altar in the Temple in Jerusalem. On the last day of
the celebration, each family baked loaves of bread
made from the newly-cut wheat and presented two
loaves in the Temple.

In his mind Paul could see those sheaves waving
before the altar. He could hear the songs of thanksgiving for the harvest. He could almost smell the
odor of freshly baked bread and see the brown loaves
as they were brought on the last day of the celebration.

In order to get to Jerusalem in time for this festival,

Paul decided not to visit Ephesus. When he found that the ship would stay several days at Miletus, only thirty miles away, he sent word to the believers in Ephesus.

Immediately some of the church people from Ephesus came to Miletus to greet the missionary who had worked in their city for three years.

Paul welcomed their visit. He told of his plan to go to Jerusalem and admitted that he felt persecution and imprisonment awaited him there. Together the friends knelt on the sand and prayed. Then they said good-by, and the Ephesians watched as Paul and his companions boarded the ship. When they could no longer see the sails, they set out to walk the thirty miles back to Ephesus.

Past little and big islands, the ship sailed before the wind, docking once on the mainland before it crossed the Mediterranean. It passed near places familiar to Paul, and as the missionaries stood on deck, he pointed out Cyprus and told Luke of his first missionary journey with Barnabas.

The ship docked at Tyre, in Syria, to unload its cargo, and Paul and his friends had a week's visit with the Christians there. They begged Paul not to go to Jerusalem, but he felt he must. When it was time to leave, mothers and fathers, and even children, followed the travelers down to the beach. Paul asked God's blessings on them and said good-by.

There was time for a day's visit with the Christians at Ptolemais, and then the ship sailed on to Caesarea.

Paul must have remembered other days in that city, but there was little time to think of the past. Philip the evangelist lived in Caesarea, and he welcomed Paul and his companions for a week's visit.

In Philip's house Paul had another warning that dangers awaited him in Jerusalem.

One day a prophet named Agabus came to Caesarea. He knew that the strict Jews in Jerusalem had never forgiven Paul for becoming a follower of the Lord Jesus. Agabus took the belt of Paul's coat and bound his own hands and feet. He showed his bonds to Paul and said, "The Holy Spirit leads me to tell you that so shall the Jews at Jerusalem bind you and deliver you to the Gentiles."

Paul's friends wept. They begged him not to go on to Jerusalem.

"You are breaking my heart with your tears," Paul told them. "Don't you know that I am ready not only to be imprisoned but even to die for my faith in the Lord Jesus?"

His friends stared at him, and they saw that his face was shining with love for his Lord. They argued no more.

"The will of the Lord be done," they said.

When it was time for Paul and his companions to leave, some of their Christian friends went with them as far as the house of Mnason, a Christian from Cyprus. There they spent the night. The next morning these friends returned home, and the travelers went on to Jerusalem. Paul's third missionary journey had ended.

28.
Trouble in Jerusalem

The narrow streets of Jerusalem were crowded when Paul and his companions reached the city. Many Jews who had come for the Passover had remained for the harvest festival of Pentecost.

Paul awoke one morning to the smell of freshly baked bread, and he knew that this was the day for presenting the loaves in the Temple. He would go there for the service after he talked with James and some of the other believers, he decided.

The Christians in Jerusalem were still meeting in the upper room, and there the believers welcomed Paul and his companions. Some of them were shocked at Paul's look of fatigue. They understood something of the reasons when Timothy told them how hard Paul had worked and some of the persecutions he had suffered.

Paul and Timothy presented the gifts from the Gentile Christians, and the Jerusalem believers received them with gratitude.

Paul then told something of the work he had been doing. The church at Jerusalem rejoiced at every report of new Christians and new churches.

"Even as far west as Corinth, there are believers in the Lord Jesus," they told each other in amazement. And they praised God for the spread of the gospel to both Jews and Gentiles.

Yet their gladness was dimmed by the fears for Paul's safety. James tried to explain the situation among the strict Jews in Jerusalem and excuse their prejudices.

"Some of them feel that you no longer respect Jewish customs," he told Paul. "Even some Jewish Christians resent the fact that you do not teach parents to circumcise their children according to the Law of Moses. I wish you could make them understand that you are loyal to the Jewish nation as well as to the Christian faith."

There was silence for a few moments. Then a man made a suggestion.

"There are four men here who have made a Jewish vow," he said. "I wonder if it might help Paul in the eyes of the strict Jews if he, too, made a vow and paid the expenses of the sacrifices not only for himself but for all five."

Paul was ready to cooperate. On the next day he went with the men to give notice of the vow whose keeping would be completed within a week. On the way to the Temple, he met an old Greek friend from Ephesus, and the two walked down the street together.

Every day Paul went to the Temple to pray and to observe the requirements of his vow. The week was almost over when trouble came. Some Jews from Ephesus recognized him as he worshiped. "I saw him walking down the street with a Gentile from our city the other day," one of them whispered. "He probably took him into the inner court with him."

The story was repeated and added to. "This Paul takes Gentiles into the Temple, even into the inner court where it is forbidden for a Gentile to enter. He is teaching men everywhere against our Law."

A mob gathered and dragged Paul out the Temple gate into the street.

"Kill him!" men shouted, and they began to beat him.

"Kill him!"

The shouts reached the ears of Claudius Lysias, the Roman tribune in the Tower of Antonia. He called soldiers and ran to the scene. As he rescued the prisoner from his tormentors, he tried to find out the charge against him. Some shouted one thing and some another, and he could not discover the facts. He ordered Paul bound with two chains and brought to the barracks in the tower.

The mob followed. When they reached the tower, they attempted to seize Paul, and the soldiers had to guard the prisoner with spears as they hurried him up the steps.

As they were about to enter, Paul turned to the officer in charge. "May I speak to you?" he asked, using the Greek language.

"Do you know Greek?" the amazed officer asked. "I thought you were that Egyptian who stirred up trouble recently and led four thousand murderers out into the wild country."

"I am a Jew," Paul replied. "I am a native of Tarsus, in Cilicia. Let me speak to these people."

The officer agreed, and Paul held up his hand for attention.

"Brethren and fathers," he began respectfully.

The mob quieted, as Paul spoke in the familiar Hebrew language.

Standing on the steps, he explained who he was and how he had been educated in Jerusalem, under Gamaliel, to be as strict a Jew as any of them. He told of persecuting the Christians in Judea and his plan

to do the same to believers in Damascus. He spoke of seeing Jesus on the road to Damascus and of Ananias who had told him he was to be God's messenger to all men.

The crowd listened, even the fiercest of the mob. Paul went on to tell of his return to Jerusalem and the vision he had as he prayed in the Temple.

"Again I saw Jesus," Paul said. "He told me to leave Jerusalem because my people there would pay no attention to my message.

"I reminded him that these people knew that I had imprisoned and beaten the believers. They had seen me standing by and approving the stoning of Stephen." Paul paused a moment, and then repeated the words Jesus had said to him, " 'Leave the city, for I will send you far away to the Gentiles.' "

At the hated word "Gentiles" the mob broke into shouts, "Away with such a fellow from the earth. He is not fit to live." They threw off their coats and pressed closer to seize Paul again.

"Take the prisoner into the barracks," the officer ordered quickly. "Flog him until he tells why the people are shouting against him."

The soldiers obeyed and bound Paul for scourging. As they did so, he turned to the captain standing by.

"Is it lawful for you to scourge a Roman citizen who has not been condemned?" he asked.

The captain held up his hand for the guards to wait. He hurried to the tribune who had given the order for scourging. "Do you know what you are doing?" he asked. "This prisoner is a Roman citizen."

The tribune went at once to Paul. "Are you really a Roman citizen?" he asked.

"Yes," Paul answered.

Claudius Lysias stared at him. "I paid a great deal of money for my citizenship," he said slowly.

Paul straightened up and threw back his shoulders. "I was born a free citizen," he said with dignity.

Frightened at what they had done, the soldiers who had bound him hurried away. The tribune, too, was afraid, for he knew he had violated one of Rome's most respected laws. The next day he ordered the chains removed from the prisoner and commanded the chief priests and the Sanhedrin to appear before him with their charges.

A prisoner, guarded by Roman soldiers, Paul faced the stern council of both Pharisees and Sadducees whom he had seen condemn Stephen to death and join in his stoning.

"Brethren," he began, "my conscience is clear before God."

The council members muttered to themselves.

"Strike him in the mouth," the high priest Ananias ordered a Temple guard.

Paul was indignant. "Do you dare act as my judge and at the same time violate the law by that order!" he accused.

"He speaks against the high priest," an onlooker shouted.

Paul realized that getting angry had not helped his case.

He looked over the crowd and remembered how the Pharisees and Sadducees argued about the resurrection. Maybe he could turn their attention to the old squabble and so get their minds off him.

"I am a Pharisee," he declared. "I am often questioned about my belief in the resurrection of the dead."

Both Sadducees and Pharisees stared at him. Then they began to argue as Paul had hoped they would. A great clamor arose, and some of the Pharisees began to defend Paul. "We see nothing wrong about this man," they said. "What if he does claim that a spirit spoke to him."

The argument grew violent. The mob pressed closer, and the tribune ordered the soldiers to take the prisoner back into the barracks.

In his cell that night, Paul was discouraged. Yet he found that his Lord was very near. He heard his voice, "Have courage, Paul. As you have witnessed to me in Jerusalem, so you will witness for me in the city of Rome."

The next morning Paul had a visitor. A relative of his had heard men plotting against the prisoner. "Forty Jews have taken an oath neither to eat nor to drink until they have killed you," the boy told Paul. "The chief priests and elders have agreed to ask the tribune to have you brought before the Sanhedrin for questioning. On the way these forty men will be waiting to ambush and kill you."

Paul thanked the boy and then called the guard. "Take this boy to the tribune," he said. "He has something important to tell him."

The guard obeyed the request, and the tribune listened carefully to the boy's story.

"Go home now," he told him. "I will take care of this matter. Tell no one that you have been talking with me."

The tribune thought about the matter and made his plans.

"Have two hundred foot soldiers and seventy horsemen and two hundred men with spears ready to leave

Jerusalem by nine o'clock tonight," he ordered his assistant. "Provide a horse for the prisoner. He must be taken safely to Felix, the Roman governor of Judea who lives in Caesarea. I will send a letter to explain the situation." The tribune began to write.

When the letter was completed, it read:

> Claudius Lysias to his Excellency, the Governor Felix: Greetings. The Jews seized this man and were about to kill him. I learned that he is a Roman citizen, so I went with my soldiers and rescued him. I wanted to know what they were accusing him of, so I took him down to their Council. I found out that he had not done a thing for which he deserved to die or be put in prison; the accusation against him had to do with questions about their own law. And when I was informed that some Jews were making a plot against him, I decided to send him to you. I told his accusers to make their charges against him before you.[29]

That night, two hundred soldiers marched from the Tower of Antonia through the dark streets of Jerusalem. With them, guarded by seventy horsemen and two hundred men with spears, rode Paul, the Apostle to the Gentiles.

29.
Under Roman Guard

As Paul rode through the darkness, under Roman guard, he had time to think what his arrest and transfer to Caesarea might mean to him.

He would be tried before Felix, the Roman governor of Judea, he realized. He knew Felix's reputation as cruel and corrupt. The governor would try to appease the Jews, but fearing Roman law, he might also refuse openly to countenance mob action. He would be influenced by Agrippa II, who was not a Jew, but who had a residence in Jerusalem and ruled as king over a large section of Palestine.

Armed peace under the Romans still prevailed in the world, and Nero had come to the throne in Rome. Paul knew that Caesarea boasted an impressive temple dedicated to the worship of the emperor. He had heard of Nero's indulgences and cruelty. There was a rumor that he had even had his own mother executed.

Paul wondered what the outcome of his trial would be. He was strangely calm, for he thought of a Ruler greater than any emperor. In his heart he heard again the reassuring words of his Lord, "You shall bear witness to me in Rome."

On through the night the prisoner and his guards rode. When they arrived in Caesarea, Paul was taken before Governor Felix, and Claudius Lysias' letter was delivered.

The governor read the tribune's letter and promised

to hear Paul's defense when the Jews came down to make their accusations. In the meantime, he ordered the accused man kept in the prison attached to the royal palace.

Five days later Ananias, the high priest, and other Jewish leaders came to Caesarea. They brought with them Tertullus to act as prosecuting attorney. He began his argument by complimenting Governor Felix and flattering him by a reference to his "wisdom" in governing Judea. Then he pointed to the prisoner.

"We have found this man a pestilent fellow," he declared. "He has stirred up trouble among the Jews all over the world and is a ringleader among the followers of a man called Jesus of Nazareth. He has insulted the Temple of the Jews."

The Jews nodded their approval.

Governor Felix turned to Paul and motioned him to speak.

"I am glad to answer these charges," Paul began, "for I know that you have been familiar with Jewish matters for some years.

"Twelve days ago I went to Jerusalem to worship, and no one can truthfully say that I made trouble there. I admit that I worship according to the teachings of Jesus Christ, and I believe in the resurrection of both the just and the unjust. It is because of this belief that these men are accusing me here."

He pointed to his enemies.

Felix was puzzled. He knew a little about the Christian faith, but he did not want to offend the high priest and his associates. "When the tribune, Claudius Lysias, comes from Jerusalem I will decide your case," he told Paul. And he gave orders that the prisoner be kept under guard and his friends be allowed to minister to him.

How grateful Paul was for those friends. Philip the evangelist, Luke, and others brought him food and saw that he had what he needed.

Yet the days were monotonous. As much as he loved the sea, Paul tired of hearing the constant washing of waves on the shore. As he watched the tides ebb and flow, he wondered how long he would have to be in prison and do no preaching.

Perhaps he spent a part of his time writing letters to the churches, for Luke and other friends had remained in Caesarea, and they helped him in every way they could.

Much of his time Paul spent preaching to his guards. He told all who would listen about the goodness of God and the wonder of faith in the Lord Jesus Christ. And through the long days and nights, the compelling urge grew in his heart, "I must preach the gospel in Rome."

When he heard that Felix was to be replaced as governor, Paul hoped for favorable action on his case, but no order for his release came. Felix, still eager to keep the favor of the Jews, sailed away from Caesarea and left Paul in prison.

"Festus is the new governor of the province," Luke told Paul one day. "He has gone to Jerusalem."

Paul knew what that visit might mean. Festus would, of course, confer with the high priest, who was appointed by the Romans. Ananias would tell his side of the story. Would Festus turn him over to the Jews? Paul wondered if Claudius Lysias was still in Jerusalem to warn the governor of the plot to kill the prisoner.

In Jerusalem the Jews made their request that Paul be brought there for trial. Festus may have suspected a plot, for he invited them to come to Caesarea and make their charges when he returned to that city.

Ten days later the Jews arrived in Caesarea, and again Paul faced his accusers.

Once more he declared himself innocent of any crime against either Jewish or Roman law.

"Do you wish to go to Jerusalem for trial?" Festus asked the prisoner, for he knew that this was what the Jews wanted.

Paul thought of the forty men who had sworn to kill him. They would never give up their attempt, he knew.

"I am here before a court of Rome," he said. "That is where I should be, for I have committed no crime against the Jews or anyone else. As a Roman citizen, I appeal to Caesar."

Festus conferred with his advisors. They knew that this meant a trial in Rome.

"You have appealed to Caesar," the governor told Paul. "To Caesar you must go. You shall be tried in Rome."

Again Paul went back to prison—to wait. What charge would Festus send with him to Rome?

One day Paul was again summoned before the governor.

"Agrippa, king of Jerusalem, is here visiting with his wife," the guard told Paul. "Festus has told Agrippa about you, and the king wants to hear what you have to say. I heard the governor say that he did not know what crime to charge you with."

The prisoner was taken to the marble audience hall of the palace. Still wearing chains on his arms, he stood before the two rulers.

Governor Festus reviewed the case and told of the prisoner's appeal to Caesar.

King Agrippa looked at the little Jew who stood

before him. "You may speak for yourself," he said. Paul began to speak, but did not ask for his release from prison. He congratulated King Agrippa on his knowledge of Jewish affairs and told of his own life as a strict Jew and a Pharisee. "I am accused because I believe in the resurrection of the dead," he declared.

Paul went on to tell of his early persecution of Christians and of the wonderful day when, as he traveled to Damascus, Jesus had spoken to him and told him to preach to the Gentiles. He told the king how he had obeyed this command in many countries and how the Jews had tried to kill him because of his witness to the Gentiles.

"I preached nothing that the old Jewish prophets did not preach," he declared. "They, too, said that the Christ must suffer and rise from the dead and proclaim light to the Gentiles."

Festus looked at the prisoner in amazement. "You are out of your mind," he said.

Paul shook his head. "I speak the truth," he said. And he turned to King Agrippa.

"Do you believe the old Jewish prophets?" he asked.

The king hesitated, and Paul went on, "I know that you do believe them."

King Agrippa rose from his seat. "You almost persuade me to become a Christian," he said.

"I wish that you and all who are here knew the joy of faith in the Lord Jesus," Paul replied.

The king turned away. The interview was finished.

As the two rulers talked the matter over, both agreed that Paul had committed no crime that deserved either death or imprisonment. And Agrippa added, "He might have been set free if he had not appealed to Caesar."

30.
Shipwrecked

At last it had been decided. Paul was to go on trial in Rome.

It was summer, probably in the year 60, that Julius, the Roman centurion, herded a group of prisoners aboard a small trading ship at the port of Caesarea. Some were men already under sentence. Some would fight with wild beasts in the arena at Rome, and their death struggles would entertain the emperor and his court.

Julius recognized that at least one prisoner was different from the others. He pointed Paul out to the ship's captain. "There is only a vague charge against this Jew," he explained. "Jewish leaders in Jerusalem accused him of breaking some religious rule. He is a Roman citizen and has appealed his case to Caesar."

"Who are the two men with him?" the captain asked. "What did they do?"

"There is no charge against them," Julius replied. "The Greek is Luke, Paul's doctor, who insisted on being allowed to care for him on the trip. The other is Aristarchus who is going along as the prisoner's servant."

The vessel was a small coastwise freighter which sailed slowly even in the best weather. The wind was against the ship on this trip, and it made even poorer time. When it docked at Tyre, Julius gave Paul and his two companions permission to go ashore. The believers welcomed the three men and ministered to them in every way that they could while the ship was in port.

As he sailed north from Tyre, Paul got a last look at the coast of Syria, and his mind traveled over the mountains to Damascus and the road where he had first seen his Lord. He thought of friends in Damascus and in Antioch. As the ship made its way around Cyprus, he recalled his first trip to that island.

Far to the north, as the vessel skirted the mainland, he could see the Taurus Mountains, and his thoughts went to his boyhood in Tarsus and on to Derbe and Lystra and other towns where he had preached. He must have told Luke some of his experiences in those places, and perhaps Luke jotted down some notes that enabled him to write so vividly about Paul's journeys.

At Myra, in Lycia, the ship docked again. Since it was bound for a port on the Adriatic and not for Rome, Julius found a grain ship from Egypt whose destination was Italy. He marched his prisoners on board.

The ship sailed for several days, making its way carefully between the islands that dotted the blue water near the coast. The wind was against it, and it made slow progress. Thus the uneasy captain changed his course and landed at Fair Havens on the island of Crete.

It was October, and under favorable circumstances, the trip would have been over and Paul in Rome.

The captain and shipowner talked with Julius about plans for the winter. Paul must have earned their respect, for he was included in the conversation.

"Most seamen consider the Mediterranean dangerous for travel after early October," Julius said thoughtfully. "Many miles of water lie between us and Italy."

Paul agreed.

"Sirs," he argued. "This is a dangerous time to sail. We will be risking much loss not only of cargo and the ship, but also of life."

The shipowner objected.

"The harbor here at Fair Havens is not a good one in which to winter," he said. "I think we can make it to Phoenix where the ship will be better protected and we can have a livelier time as we wait."

"Phoenix is on this same island, isn't it?" asked Julius.

The shipowner nodded. "It's not far," he said. "We should make it in less than a day." Julius agreed to the plan to sail for Phoenix.

A light wind was blowing from the south the next morning, and the captain of the ship ordered the anchor lifted. Not waiting to hoist the little boat attached to a line, the ship scurried out of the harbor and around a small point of land. It headed west around the coast for Phoenix. Behind, the little boat bobbed up and down on the waves.

Suddenly the wind changed to a blow from the north. Black clouds filled the sky, and lightning flashed.

"Undergird the ship," the captain ordered. "From the looks of the skies, a bad storm is on the way."

The wind was increasing. Though it had already driven the vessel off its course, near the island of Clauda, land sheltered the ship enough for the sailors to fasten the heavy, thick cables around the hull. They could hardly draw up the little boat which had been towed behind.

Stronger and stronger the wind blew, and the little

island no longer broke its force. Fearing that the ship might be driven into the treacherous quicksands of North Africa, the captain ordered the gear lowered. Now the wind drove the ship, not toward the south, but west into the open sea.

Harder and harder the wind blew. The storm was a northeaster, feared by every wise seaman. Huge waves tossed the vessel from side to side. Higher and higher they rose and crashed on the deck, leaving it covered with foam.

The captain gave orders to lighten the cargo, and the sailors threw heavy sacks of wheat overboard.

Three days later, to lighten the load even more, they threw the tackling overboard.

Hours and days passed, and still the storm raged. For days there was darkness. There was no sign of the sun or even of a star in the sky. No one thought of food. Officers, sailors, and prisoners gave up any idea of survival. They huddled together, waiting for death.

One man alone had hope. Paul had been thinking and praying. One night he spoke to his frightened fellow travelers.

"Men," he said, "we should not have set sail from Crete, yet I tell you to take heart. The ship will be destroyed, but there will be no loss of life."

The sailors and even Julius, the centurion, stared at the prisoner. "How does he know?" they muttered.

Paul went on. "The God to whom I belong and whom I worship has sent me a message.

" 'Do not be afraid, Paul,' the messenger assured me. 'You will yet stand before Caesar, and God has heard your prayer that no man on the ship shall be lost.' "

Paul waited a moment. Then he added, with confidence, "I have faith in God that all this is true. We will be shipwrecked on some island."

More days and nights of darkness passed, and still the storm continued. The waves tossed the ship as if it were a light toy.

The ship was fourteen nights out of port when a keen-eared sailor caught the noise of breakers.

Realizing that land must be near, he let down a rope with a lead weight on the end to measure the depth of the water. He found a measure of twenty fathoms, about one hundred and twenty feet. A little later he sounded again and found a depth of only fifteen fathoms.

"We are approaching land," he reported.

Fearing that the ship might run onto rocks, the captain ordered four anchors dropped from the stern of the vessel and waited for daybreak.

As gray light touched the thick darkness, Paul looked about him and saw that the ship was not far from a rocky coast. He saw also that the sailors were lowering a boat and were about to desert the ship. He knew the need for those sailors and hurried to Julius.

"Unless these men remain in the ship, we cannot be saved," he said, and the centurion ordered the ropes to the boat cut.

Paul looked up at the sky and found one spot that seemed a bit lighter than the rest.

Again he spoke to his companions. "It has been two weeks since the storm began," he said. "You have not even thought of food. Eat something to give you strength."

Before their amazed eyes, he calmly took a piece of bread, broke it into pieces and thanked God for it. Then he passed it to the cowering men. He himself began to eat.

The sailors were encouraged. They, too, ate.

Then they threw the last of the dripping cargo overboard.

Dawn came, and the clouds still hung heavy. Yet the sailors could faintly see a small bay and a rocky beach. They pulled up the anchors and hoisted the sail. The wind was still strong, and Paul was not surprised when the vessel struck a shoal and ran aground. Pounded by the surf, the ship began to break into pieces.

The guards hurried to Julius. "The prisoners will escape," they warned, "and we will pay the penalty with our lives. Give us permission to kill them."

Julius hesitated for a moment. Then he looked at Paul and shook his head.

"No," he said, and he ordered the prisoners who could swim to throw themselves overboard and head for land.

"Cling to planks or whatever you can find," he told the others.

The ship had broken into pieces now, and the men were in the water, doing their best to reach land.

When at last they stood on shore, Julius counted two hundred seventy-six persons, every man who had been on board.

"Where are we?" he asked a native who had run down to the shore.

"On the island of Melita," the man replied.

Luke himself tells this story in the twenty-seventh chapter of the Book of Acts. Read it and decide whether you agree with one writer who calls it "one of the best sea tales of antiquity."

31.
Rome at Last

On any world map of the first century A.D., including those in this book, is the island where Paul's ship was wrecked. On modern maps, it is not labeled *Melita*, but *Malta*. In this chapter, it is called the island of Malta.

In the Acts of the Apostles, Luke calls the natives of Malta "barbarians," but to him that term meant only that they were not Greeks. Archaeologists now say that these people of Malta spoke a language so much resembling Hebrew that Paul was able to talk with them.

These natives were quick to help the shivering men whom the waves had cast upon their shores. It was cold and rainy, and immediately they kindled a fire on the beach.

Paul busied himself gathering brush for the fire. As he fed the wood to the flames, a viper, aroused by the heat, crawled out and fastened on his hand. He shook it off and stirred the fire. The natives stared, expecting his arm to begin to swell.

"He may fall dead," one of them whispered. "Perhaps he is a murderer who has escaped the sea and is getting his punishment this way."

Paul went on with his work, and when the natives saw that nothing was happening to him, they changed their minds and declared that he was a god.

Paul sighed and remembered the procession that had tried to worship Barnabas and himself at Lystra on their first missionary journey. "People are much alike in all places," he said to himself. And he went on helping his companions dry their clothes.

"Have you seen the governor of the island?" a man asked the centurion Julius the next day. Julius shook his head. "Does he live near here?" he asked.

The man pointed to a grove of trees back from the beach. "His plantation begins there," he replied. "His old father who lives with him is quite sick."

Julius had seen Paul help sick people on the voyage. He took him along when he went to call on the governor, and they stayed in his home three days.

Paul visited the sick man and prayed for him, putting his hands on him with a healing touch.

When the island people heard that the governor's father was well again, they brought sick members of their own families to Paul, and they were healed. For three months the shipwrecked men stayed on the island of Malta.

When springtime came, Julius found another ship from Egypt. It had wintered in a cove of the island, and it was bound for Italy. On its prow was the name *Castor and Pollux* which meant *Twin Brothers*. These were the patron gods of both Greek and Roman sailors.

Julius rounded up his prisoners and marched them toward the ship. As they came down to the beach, the natives of Malta followed Paul with all sorts of gifts. They thanked him for helping so many of their people.

On a calm sea the *Twin Brothers* sailed to Syracuse, on the coast of Sicily. There it docked for three days. Paul and his friends had time to go ashore and see the old temple of Athena which had been built almost five hundred years before.

When they were back on board, the ship sailed north and touched at the port of Rhegium, on the southern tip of the boot-shaped mainland of Italy. From there, it was only a day's sail along the coast to Puteoli, the principal port for ships carrying cargoes of grain to Rome.

The wind was from the south when the *Twin Brothers* left Rhegium, and Paul saw the deep blue waters of the Mediterranean and the long stretches of the green coast of Italy. Beyond the lowlands, he glimpsed tall mountains. He knew that the ranges extended for miles north and beyond those rugged peaks lay the city of Rome. He lifted his hands to shade his eyes. Above the clanking of his chains, he seemed to hear again the words with which his Lord had twice encouraged him, "Fear not, Paul. As you have testified of me in Jerusalem, so you must bear witness to me in Rome."

As the ship made its way slowly through the bay and into the port of Puteoli, Paul saw fishermen with their nets working the oyster beds which lay nearby. He noticed that the harbor was full of ships—freighters, and pleasure crafts with brightly colored sails. When the vessel docked, Paul was surprised to see people smiling and waving at him.

"We are believers," they introduced themselves. "We heard you were arriving and have come to meet you." They begged him to visit them. Perhaps Julius wanted to see the famous games and races which were in progress in the spring, for he allowed Paul and his companions to remain in Puteoli for a week; then he faced his prisoners toward Rome.

"We will follow the main road north to Capua,"

he explained. "There it connects with the Appian Way."

Paul and his companions marched through little towns and across rushing streams of water. They saw hills covered with vineyards and tall trees beginning to bud. When they reached the Appian Way, they found more traffic on the road. They met wealthy senators riding on richly decorated litters carried on the shoulders of four men. They saw by the roadside luxurious villas and well-kept gardens with marble statues of the gods of Rome.

At the Forum of Appius, Paul and his companions had another surprise. The believers in Rome had heard of Paul's arrival in Italy and had come to meet him. They appreciated the letter he had written to them and welcomed him to their fellowship. Paul was delighted to recognize some Christians from cities where he had preached. He thanked God and took courage. Another group of believers met the prisoner at the point called *Three Taverns*.

The guards looked on in astonishment. "What kind of prisoner is this?" they asked.

Julius shook his head. "In all my years, I have never seen one like this Paul," he said. "He has helped everybody on this trip. When we were shipwrecked, his thought was only for his companions, even the worst of the prisoners. The governor of Malta found him so interesting that he kept him visiting in his palace for three days."

Julius pointed to the Christians from Rome. "See how these people love him!" he said. "Who are they?"

One of the Christians heard the question and replied, "We, too, are believers in the Lord Jesus Christ."

Rome was in sight now, but there was no time for

Paul and his companions even to glimpse the magnificence of the Pantheon or the amphitheater. Julius hurried his prisoners through the gates and down the street to the prison. There he delivered them to new guards. Before he left, he told Paul good-by, and Paul thanked him for his kindness on the trip.

Since the charge against Paul was very indefinite, he was allowed to rent a house and live there. He was, however, a prisoner chained constantly to a Roman soldier. Yet he was in the city where he had so much wanted to be—in the Imperial Capital, Rome.

As he made his plans, his thoughts turned again to his own people, the Jews. He sent for some of their leaders and told them of his situation. "The Romans would have released me in Caesarea," he said, "but the Jews from Jerusalem objected. Yet I make no charge against my nation. It is really for Israel's hope of the Messiah that I am bound by these chains. For I am a follower of the Lord Jesus Christ."

"We have received no report on you from Jerusalem," the Roman Jews declared, "but we have heard much evil of the Christian Way which you follow. We will be glad to hear your views."

Every day for some time, these Jews came to Paul's house, and he spoke to them about the Lord Jesus Christ, giving them the same gospel message he had preached wherever he went. "The Lord Jesus was crucified, but God raised him from the dead. He is the Messiah, long promised to the Jewish nation."

The Jews listened carefully. Some of them became believers; others did not.

One day Paul faced the fact that not many Jews would accept the gospel. Sadly he quoted the words of an ancient prophet:

Because this people's minds are dull,
        they have stopped up their ears,
        and have closed their eyes.
Otherwise, their eyes would see,
        their ears would hear,
        their minds would understand,
and they would turn to me, says God,
        and I would heal them.[30]

And he added what he had said so often in the
synagogues of the Jews: "You are to know, then, that
God's message of salvation has been sent to the Gentiles. They will listen!" [31]

Yet Paul did not stop witnessing to his Lord. He
gave the gospel message to the soldiers who guarded
him and to their friends whom they brought to hear
him. Many of them became believers, some even "of
Caesar's household." The Christians visited him too,
and he taught them more about the way followers of
Jesus must live. They, too, brought friends to hear
him.

One of Paul's visitors was a runaway Greek slave
named Onesimus. Paul told the young man about the
Lord Jesus Christ, and Onesimus became a believer.

Paul knew that Roman law allowed a runaway
slave to be beaten, branded, or even killed. But he
also knew that a Christian must be honest. He faced
Onesimus with this obligation. He did something else,
too. He wrote a letter to Onesimus' master whom he
had once known. In that letter he urged his friend
to receive Onesimus not as a slave but as a brother
in Christ. "I will pay whatever he owes you," Paul
promised. "I know you will do even more than I ask."

You can find all of Paul's letter about Onesimus

in your Bible. It is called The Letter of Paul to Philemon.

Paul wrote other letters while he was in prison, telling Luke the words to put on paper. He wrote to the Christians in Philippi and in Colosse and possibly in other places. Many of Paul's letters are in the Bible. Through them, he is still preaching the gospel of the Lord Jesus.

Luke watched the events of that first imprisonment in Rome. He closes the Book of Acts with a summary of those days in Rome:

> For two years Paul lived there in a place he rented for himself, and welcomed all who came to see him. He preached about the Kingdom of God and taught about the Lord Jesus Christ, speaking with all boldness and freedom.[32]

32.
When Paul Faced Death

In A.D. 64, the city of Rome lay in ruins. Not one of its seven hills had escaped the great fire. The stones that remained were still dark with smoke and charred timbers when Emperor Nero began to do two things.

First he set about rebuilding the city. For himself he erected a great golden palace, said to be the finest in the world.

Then, he had to find someone to blame for the burning of Rome. The followers of a new religion had come to his attention. Some of the soldiers in his own army had become believers in one whom they called Jesus the Christ. They were refusing to join in the immoralities common in the city, and they would have no part in the worship of the emperor.

Few of the Christians were rich. Most of them did not hold high positions. Many were Jews, and the Romans disliked the Jews. But worst of all, these Christians refused to worship the Roman emperor as the government ordered them to do. Such refusal was crime enough for Nero. He began to speak of this refusal as treason to Rome, and he ordered the arrest of such traitors.

Rumors and charges spread, and the hunt began. Throughout the city, in the neighboring countryside, and in many other parts of the empire, believers were arrested and put to death when they refused to compromise their faith in the Lord Jesus Christ.

In Rome, many Christians were thrown to lions in the arena. Sometimes they were tied to posts and trees, and oil was poured over their clothing. The flames of their burning leaped high like torches on a dark night. Even Roman citizens who were Christians did not escape but were beheaded. The persecution continued.

One day an old man was arrested and brought to the prison in Rome. A guard recognized him.

"He is that same preacher who was a prisoner in this city several years ago," the guard declared. "He was always talking about Jesus Christ whom these Christians worship as their God."

The prisoner lifted his head and looked the guard straight in the face. "Yes," he said, "I am Paul, a servant of the Lord Jesus Christ. I am also a Roman citizen."

"Take him to the dungeon," the guard ordered, and Paul was taken to a dark, stone cell, usually reserved for the worst criminals.

He shivered in the damp winter air. There was no heat in the cell, and only a dim light filtered through the high barred window. He was tired, and his chains were heavy.

Paul thought of the sunny courtyard of his first imprisonment and of the friends who had ministered to him. He wished for his books and for the warm coat he had left with a friend in Troas.

"Luke will get to me somehow," he assured himself. "He has stood by me faithfully in all my troubles."

One day Luke did come, and Paul welcomed him gratefully.

"What news do you bring of the believers?" Paul asked.

Luke shook his head.

"There is little to tell that is good," he said. "Persecutions have spread all over the empire."

"Are the Christians denying their faith?" Paul asked.

Luke smiled. "No," he said. "Most of them are true to their Lord. Here in Rome they meet in caves in spite of the emperor's orders, but daily there are arrests and tortures. How is it here in prison?"

"More prisoners are brought in every day," Paul answered sadly, "and old ones are dragged out to die for their faith. I will not be here much longer."

Luke put his hand on the old man's shoulder. "You have done a great work for the Lord Jesus," he told his friend. "Think of the Christians in Judea and Syria, in Galatia, in Phrygia, in Macedonia, and in Greece. You have preached the gospel in almost all the world—even here in Rome."

Paul smiled. "Our Lord has been good to me," he said. "In spite of the fact that I once persecuted his followers, he trusted me to preach the gospel to both Jews and Gentiles. He gave me many friends, but most of them are far away. My Lord has always stood by me and strengthened me. He will never fail me."

Paul paused. Then he lifted a chained hand and went on:

I know whom I have believed, and am persuaded that he is able to keep that which I have committed unto him against that day.[33]

ROMANS
CORINTHIANS
PHILEMON
TIMOTHY
EPHESIANS
GALATIANS
PHILIPPIANS
TITUS
THESSALONIANS
COLOSSIANS

"I am not ashamed of the gospel of Christ, though I am a prisoner for preaching it. It is still the power of God unto salvation to every one who trusts the Lord Jesus Christ."

Luke stirred from his seat. "I do not know how long I will be allowed to stay with you," he said. "What can I do for you today?"

"I want to write to Timothy," Paul replied. "I love him like a son. Every day I thank God for him—and for you too, Luke."

Luke's hand was trembling as he opened the bag which he carried and produced parchment, ink, and writing brush. He began to write as Paul directed him.

Paul told Timothy how much he wanted to see him and reminded him not to be afraid. He dictated:

God hath not given us the spirit of fear; but
of power, and of love, and of a sound mind.[34]

A bit of gray light from the barred window fell on the floor of the cell. The stones reminded Paul of the broad rocks which paved the wide road outside the city. He thought of the believers who were being executed beside that road, and he knew that the time of his own death was near.

He spoke in a firm voice as he finished his letter.

I am now ready to be offered,
And the time of my departure is at hand.
I have fought a good fight,
I have finished my course,
I have kept the faith:
Henceforth there is laid up for me a crown of
righteousness,

Which the Lord, the righteous judge, shall
   give me
At that day:
And not to me only,
But unto all them also that love his appear-
   ing.[35]

No record of the death of Paul has yet been dis-
covered, but a story has come down through the centuries that he was beheaded outside the city of Rome.

Great buildings have been erected in Rome and
other cities in memory of the Apostle to the Gentiles,
but two very different monuments stand tall today
to honor him before all the world.

One is the faith which he lived and preached. The
other is the collection of letters which the Spirit of
God inspired him to write. Through those letters,
preserved in the Bible, Paul is still witnessing to his
Lord.

Bible References

All Scripture quotations are from *Good News for Modern Man,* Today's English Version of the New Testament and Psalms, unless otherwise marked. Those marked RSV are from the Revised Standard Version; those marked KJV are from the King James Version; and those marked ASV are from the American Standard Version.

Footnote Number	Page Number	Book of Bible
1	10	Acts 21:39
2	10	Acts 22:3
3	10	Acts 22:28, KJV
4	10	Galatians 1:14
5	15	Genesis 1:1, 16–18, RSV
6	17	Deuteronomy 6:4–5, RSV
7	20	Deuteronomy 6:4–5, RSV
8	38	Deuteronomy 33:12, RSV
9	43	Psalm 147:1, 4–5
10	44	Psalm 107:23–26, 28–30
11	45	Ezekiel 27:2–9, RSV
12	49	Psalm 122:1–2
13	51	Psalm 125:2
14	61	Deuteronomy 13:8–10, ASV
15	69	Deuteronomy 13:8–10, ASV
16	86	Galatians 1:16–17
17	94	Galatians 1:18–24
18	110	Acts 13:47, RSV
19	110	Matthew 28:20, RSV